Puzzles for
Mindfulness

WORDSEARCH

Puzzles for Mindfulness

WORDSEARCH

Enjoy some time out with
these relaxing puzzles

SIRIUS

SIRIUS

This edition published in 2022 by Sirius Publishing, a division of
Arcturus Publishing Limited,
26/27 Bickels Yard, 151–153 Bermondsey Street,
London SE1 3HA

ISBN: 978-1-3988-1947-4
AD010384NT

Printed in China

1   GREAT Start

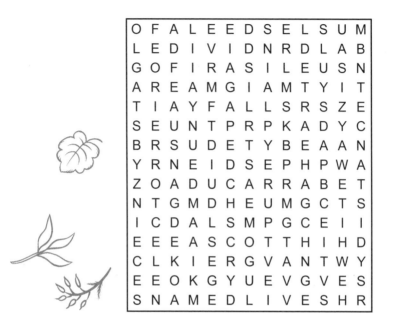

```
O F A L E E D S E L S U M
L E D I V I D N R D L A B
G O F I R A S I L E U S N
A R E A M G I A M T Y I T
T I A Y F A L L S R S Z E
S E U N T P R P K A D Y C
B R S U D E T Y B E A A N
Y R N E I D S E P H P W A
Z O A D U C A R R A B E T
N T G M D H E U M G C T S
I C D A L S M P G C E I I
E E E A S C O T T H I H D
C L K I E R G V A N T W Y
E E O K G Y U E V G V E S
S N A M E D L I V E S H R
```

- BARRACUDA
- BASIN
- DEPRESSION
- DISTANCE
- DIVIDE
- EGRET
- ELECTOR
- FALLS
- GATSBY
- GRAND-DAUGHTER
- HEARTED
- LAKES
- MOGUL
- NIECE
- PLAINS
- PYRAMID
- SCOTT
- WHITE WAY

2   Waterfalls

```
S I Y A M E P R E O B U N
H Z E Y D A Y H S F S U A
O A S P I D S S A A E L S
S R M M Z Q O I V N E X M
H A E X O F R A W G T I F
O T Y Y G O H O U Y N O Q
N U T N T M R T U N P W M
E M A C M B S E E R C N E
L L I H C R U H C X T U S
H V H A Y I A Z B O N O U
E R I H R H J Z L N V T O
R Q H T A L M M I R K E L
I U E I T G E A N O P P A
P L A N N R I N K A S O P
R E T A W E T I H W P H E
```

- BROWNE
- CHURCHILL
- HAVASU
- HOPETOUN
- KRIMML
- LANGFOSS
- MINNEHAHA
- MOORE COVE
- MUTARAZI
- PALOUSE
- PHANTOM
- RHINE
- RINKA
- SHOSHONE
- TOLMER
- TUGELA
- VICTORIA
- WHITEWATER

Mindfulness is not
chasing the moment
but beautifying
the moment.

Amit Ray

3　Farm Animals

S	E	S	P	I	T	A	N	A	R	S	T	E
S	I	R	G	O	O	B	S	F	N	A	H	T
E	V	S	L	N	N	B	Y	O	Y	J	K	D
S	S	E	B	V	I	I	I	U	E	I	I	C
E	B	V	B	U	G	L	E	H	D	W	I	A
E	M	L	A	J	L	U	S	S	V	E	E	R
G	A	A	B	A	R	L	V	O	G	A	S	S
P	L	C	T	A	Z	A	O	S	G	O	S	O
S	J	S	M	I	E	S	Y	C	I	F	D	C
E	R	S	D	A	E	P	R	S	K	N	E	T
K	M	C	J	E	C	J	P	E	S	S	X	P
A	K	G	A	N	D	E	R	S	W	I	T	I
R	W	E	U	T	E	I	N	R	O	R	E	X
D	J	Y	V	H	S	X	A	O	S	G	I	P
K	D	C	S	H	A	V	E	H	G	A	R	N

- BULLOCKS
- CALVES
- CATS
- DOGS
- DRAKES
- EWES
- GANDERS
- GEESE
- GOSLINGS
- HORSES
- KIDS
- LAMBS
- PIGS
- PONIES
- RAMS
- SHEEP
- SOWS
- STALLIONS

4 Cakes

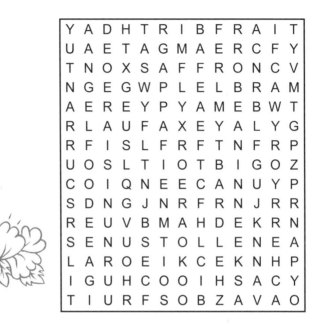

```
Y A D H T R I B F R A I T
U A E T A G M A E R C F Y
T N O X S A F F R O N C V
N G E G W P L E L B R A M
A E R E Y P Y A M E B W T
R L A U F A X E Y A L Y G
R F I S L F R F T N F R P
U O S L T I O T B I G O Z
C O I Q N E E C A N U Y P
S D N G J N R F R N J R R
R E U V B M A H D E K R N
S E N U S T O L L E N E A
L A R O E I K C E K N H P
I G U H C O O I H S A C Y
T I U R F S O B Z A V A O
```

- ANGEL FOOD
- BATTENBURG
- BIRTHDAY
- CHERRY
- COFFEE
- CREAM GATEAU
- CURRANT
- EASTER
- FRUIT
- LAYER
- MARBLE
- MERINGUE
- MOCHA
- POUND
- RAISIN
- SAFFRON
- SCONES
- STOLLEN

5 Mindfulness

N	V	T	N	E	M	O	M	E	H	T	N	I
O	E	S	T	A	G	E	E	U	L	Y	A	E
I	J	A	R	C	L	A	C	H	R	T	E	C
T	T	K	E	J	E	L	R	A	K	L	R	N
A	R	I	W	S	A	P	U	U	U	T	U	E
L	H	F	M	R	U	T	S	F	O	M	S	D
P	I	T	I	E	C	C	T	E	Z	C	O	N
M	U	T	M	N	L	H	O	M	R	E	P	E
E	Y	G	A	R	G	E	O	F	B	D	M	C
T	N	S	N	U	A	D	S	B	A	R	O	S
N	N	E	O	I	S	W	E	S	J	A	C	N
O	O	H	R	I	N	P	E	A	N	G	A	A
C	T	A	W	G	Y	E	A	P	M	E	Z	R
A	S	M	U	N	Y	G	P	C	E	R	S	T
I	U	Q	U	I	E	T	R	O	E	S	A	S

- CLARITY
- COMPOSURE
- CONTEM-PLATION
- COURAGE
- ENERGY
- FOCUS
- IN THE MOMENT
- OPENING UP
- QUIET
- REGARD
- RESPECT
- SANCTUARY
- SPACE
- THOUGHTFUL
- TIMELESSNESS
- TRAN-SCENDENCE
- WARMTH
- WISDOM

6   EARTH Words

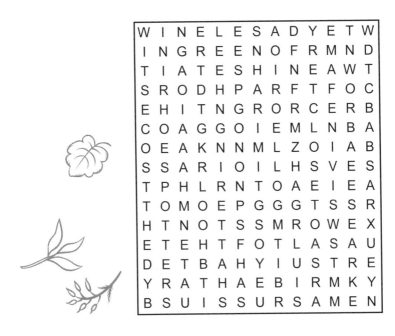

```
W I N E L E S A D Y E T W
I N G R E E N O F R M N D
T I A T E S H I N E A W T
S R O D H P A R F T F O C
E H I T N G R O R C E R B
C O A G G O I E M L N B A
O E A K N N M L Z O I A B
S S A R I O I L H S V E S
T P H L R N T O A E I E A
T O M O E P G G G T S S R
H T N O T S S M R O W E X
E T E H T F O T L A S A U
D E T B A H Y I U S T R E
Y R A T H A E B I R M K Y
B S U I S S U R S A M E N
```

- ALMOND
- BOARD
- BROWN
- CLOSET
- COST THE
- GOING TO

- GREEN
- LIGHT
- MOTHER
- MOVER
- POTTER'S
- RARE

- SALT OF THE
- SHAKING
- SHATTERING
- SHINE
- TREMOR
- WORMS

7 HOUSE Words

```
C E D S S T E R A R R J S
O U H E W E W C E M A R N
F N L L E D M O R B U E A
J U E U V N I T R A M A K
R A D G M O O R V R F R E
M O L C B R E A G W A T Z
G O E G T T M A I D B P S
N H Y N N H C D E F E T S
I F E U T F H A S V B K D
K G H B M O L S U L O E L
A W U W V E V Y O T U E O
E G G N O V E E M K N P H
R E W Y O R A S E O D E E
B R E I C P K E B A J R T
F A F B U I L D E R U T S
```

- AGENT
- BOUND
- BREAKING
- BUILDER
- CRAFT
- FLY
- HOLD
- HUNTER
- KEEPER
- LEEK
- MAID
- MARTIN
- MOUSE
- ROOM
- RULES
- SNAKE
- SPARROW
- WORK

8   Saints

```
F R A O F M A U R U S E J
V T H O M A S A W B S Q W
G N N U R A K E J U S F E
A D P E L T H R S E H Y M
U E A K C T Q D E H Q S O
D R R O T N N N Y G U E L
E F H A Q I I A Q N B T O
N I M X H T C V I R Q H H
T N R T N I S C A D W E T
I I I E N U I B E O E L R
U W L T T S D D Q R R B A
S A H N R E I L E H D U B
V E Y U W E P T A R N R E
O U D U L F U S E E A G E
U R E R A H C S N A G A Q
```

- ANDREA
- ANDREW
- ANSCHAR
- BARBE
- BARTH-
  OLOMEW
- ETHELBURGA

- GAUDENTIUS
- HELIER
- HYACINTHE
- MATTHEW
- MAURUS
- PETER

- SWITHIN
- THOMAS
- URSICINUS
- VALENTINE
- VINCENT
- WINIFRED

9 Fashion Designers

```
T E R I S A T E Y V L T Y
C T P S E R Y Y E F O N R
A N M S O U V A A V U A B
N E U I K M H U D P B U E
K R D I R I C C I M O Q W
B U R D V M W D G T U N J
I A Y D O H T R O W T I V
N L L L U O E H U G I O R
S T O E I E W F L M N O N
D N L F N F T T J Y L G A
E I G R C C M D S W A R E
N A R E A M I E S E G I G
A S W G S E M A J U W A T
M E P A A G U T G C H O O
S I L L E N I D R A C M D
```

- AMIES
- BALENCIAGA
- CARDIN
- CHOO
- DIOR
- ELLIS
- GREEN
- JAMES
- LAGERFELD
- LOUBOUTIN
- MUIR
- QUANT
- RICCI
- SAINT LAURENT
- VUITTON
- WESTWOOD
- WORTH
- YUKI

10 Japan

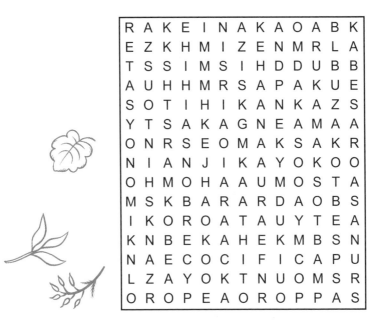

```
R A K E I N A K A O A B K
E Z K H M I Z E N M R L A
T S S I M S I H D D U B B
A U H H M R S A P A K U E
S O T I H I K A N K A Z S
Y T S A K A G N E A M A A
O N R S E O M A K S A K R
N I A N J I K A Y O K O O
O H M O H A A U M O S T A
M S K B A R A R D A O B S
I K O R O A T A U Y T E A
K N B E K A H E K M B S N
N A E C O C I F I C A P U
L Z A Y O K T N U O M S R
O R O P E A O R O P P A S
```

- AKIHITO
- BONSAI
- BUDDHISM
- HAMAMATSU
- KAMAKURA
- KIMIGAYO
- KIMONO
- KOBE
- KYOTO
- MOUNT KOYA
- OKAZU
- OSAKA
- PACIFIC OCEAN
- SAMURAI
- SAPPORO
- SHIKOKU
- SHINTO
- SUSHI

11 Rock and Pop Groups

```
R E L T A S O R E S A M M
S A P E X P O T Z Z E N M
C A S N B A N E R N I A O
U R I A H H E E P M B K H
E F E U Q C E H E A M E A
X C H I C A G O Y E F U S
I R O N B U T T E R F L Y
L A E X K U U S E C C T I
E T Z Y R U D E M A S Y R
C F S T A T U S Q U O A G
S X L S E V P U A M R I T
T E L S H E R B E T K E A
S O C L O U T U K S U B S
F T T Y C A Y C E H B P L
I D B O E E B F R A D E C
```

- ABBA
- CHICAGO
- CLOUT
- CREAM
- EXILE
- FREE

- INXS
- IRON BUTTERFLY
- SHERBET
- STATUS QUO
- STYX
- TEN CC

- TOTO
- T'PAU
- TURTLES
- UK SUBS
- URIAH HEEP
- ZZ TOP

12   Fruits

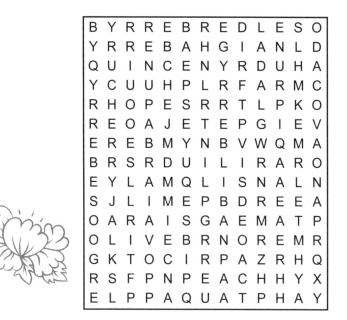

```
B Y R R E B R E D L E S O
Y R R E B A H G I A N L D
Q U I N C E N Y R D U H A
Y C U U H P L R F A R M C
R H O P E S R R T L P K O
R E O A J E T E P G I E V
E R E B M Y N B V W Q M A
B R S R D U I L I R A R O
E Y L A M Q L I S N A L N
S J L I M E P B D R E E A
O A R A I S G A E M A T P
O L I V E B R N O R E M R
G K T O C I R P A Z R H Q
R S F P N P E A C H H Y X
E L P P A Q U A T P H A Y
```

- APPLE
- APRICOT
- AVOCADO
- BILBERRY
- CHERRY
- ELDERBERRY

- GOOSEBERRY
- GRAPE
- KIWI
- LIME
- MANDARIN
- MULBERRY

- OLIVE
- PEACH
- PEAR
- POMELO
- PRUNE
- QUINCE

13   Summer

```
R K N N I C S H O R T S I
C A M P I N G V C E N U J
Z S N N X G N I O A V Y U
B N C O B R N E G Z E F J
B I N D I A E I L T C B W
P A K H A T N X F L R X G
P E R I X L A D P R O W E
K A R B N B A C S S U P U
H N R R E I L S A T G S W
T H C A Y C A D A V A A W
M R T U S U U H I O S N W
R I D G V O Z E V P E A D
A M N U N D L U S G S E H
W S E S O R E P P P Y M E
Z D W T M E V A W T A E H
```

- AUGUST
- BANDSTAND
- BARBECUE
- BEACH
- BIKINI
- CAMPING
- HEATWAVE
- PARASOL
- PICNIC
- POLLEN
- ROSES
- SALAD
- SHORTS
- SURFING
- VACATION
- WARMTH
- WASPS
- YACHT

14   Creatures' Features

```
S T H O R E S L L E H S N
T R E U A C V A S P E B A
I S E R U L E N P V N E P
N I S G N A F Q O O G O Y
G R E A C W V O T N U S N
T S S D S S H E S V N C Q
T E N T A C L E S O X I H
F N E L G E W E U L T A R
E I W F K O L T A E L I E
L P W S D A E H O R N S E
Y S O C C E L Z Z U M R S
A X F S R A B D O M E N B
E V A S E R A B I R E N N
L Y Q U A S I K E R I N E
U X A R O H T E A W A S I
```

- ABDOMEN
- CLAWS
- EXOSKELETON
- FANGS
- HEAD
- HOOVES
- HORNS
- MUZZLE
- POUCH
- SCALES
- SHELL
- SNOUT
- SPINES
- SPOTS
- STING
- TENTACLES
- THORAX
- WEBBED FEET

15 Ready

```
D O H E D I P A R L O Y S
S H E L P E N C D V G I D
C H A O S P N E G T U M E
F O A J W W R N P I O B N
D W M R K A I U A R A S I
I E C P P L T F Y L E I L
R L S E L K B K T N P E C
I E R I E E Y Y O A V L N
G P W E O L T D R I K E I
G O N P E P W E N E S P O
E S F M D A L E D Y B E U
D R I N O R D E R N P H T
O T X O V V S Y U L D S F
U A E R A Y D E E P S I N
T U D Y E G N E O E T W Z
```

- COMPLETED
- DONE
- FIT
- FIXED
- IN ORDER
- INCLINED

- KEEN
- PLANNED
- POISED
- PREPARED
- RAPID
- RIGGED OUT

- SET
- SHARP
- SPEEDY
- SWIFT
- TIMELY
- WILLING

The principle of
nowness is very
important to any
effort to establish an
enlightened society.

Pema Chödrön

16 Written by Hand

```
D I G I I T E M E N A D E
Y R K N L A N R U O J G R
A J A W I N T E F R A E M
S I I C B T S A E S B E U
E L N K S A E D S M R R D
L A A V Z A N E U W E U N
A B T E I I M N R R P V A
U E A L M T E T E G O C R
T L S E S N A C S R R E O
O E R I O Y E T E I T R M
G V X H R I A S I T R G E
R E P A P M A X E O T H M
A Y I T E I B L P N N O C
P D E U S A B P N A R E T
H N O I T P I R C S E R P
```

- AUTOGRAPH

- BANNER

- CHRISTMAS CARD

- DIARY

- EXAM PAPER

- GREETING

- INVITATION

- JOURNAL

- LABEL

- LETTER

- MEMORAN-DUM

- MESSAGE

- PHONE NUMBER

- PRESCRIPTION

- RECEIPT

- REMINDER

- REPORT

- WILL

17 Capital Cities of the Americas

```
S N W O T E G R O E G A S
E A I Y B B M Z X I C O A
R S N E T I R A O J O V O
I U S J S I R A N C C G I
A N G A U O C A S A N P L
S C C E N A J A M I G H M
O I A A N T N N M A L U G
N O R H Y D I O A A R I A
E N A A I E D A B S N A A
U B C V C O N H G B H A P
B X A A T T B N O O U A P
E P S N I D A G E T R E O
K R A A A Y O Q U I T O T
N S D E O T T A W A V R S
S R O D A V L A S N A S E
```

- ASUNCION
- BOGOTA
- BRASILIA
- BUENOS AIRES
- CARACAS
- CAYENNE
- GEORGETOWN
- HAVANA
- MANAGUA
- OTTAWA
- PANAMA CITY
- PARAMARIBO
- QUITO
- SAN JOSE
- SAN JUAN
- SAN SALVADOR
- SANTIAGO
- SANTO DOMINGO

18 Human Characters

```
A E F I E D D L E R E L Y
R X T V C M S A D I S T W
E T A I I A V Y E R U R O
H N S S A R V I A A E S
K O E I N A J P E W S M E
P R O D T N R B E O T A F
H Y A L C A E A F R S E A
A L W S I C M C P T I R R
R R C T O G P G T H M D D
R E K O J M A A A Y I Y E
I E T N A S A N E R T A I
D A B D N O G A R A P D C
A B M B R I U D E R O L A
N A S F I N E T E R N D E
N Y H G F F N A I F F U R
```

- BEAUTY
- CARPER
- DAYDREAMER
- FIBBER
- HARRIDAN
- HOOLIGAN

- JOKER
- KNAVE
- MADMAN
- MISER
- OPTIMIST
- PARAGON

- PARASITE
- PRAGMATIST
- RUFFIAN
- SADIST
- VANDAL
- WORTHY

19 Ability

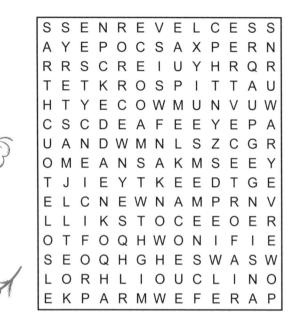

```
S S E N R E V E L C E S S
A Y E P O C S A X P E R N
R R S C R E I U Y H R Q R
T E T K R O S P I T T A U
H T Y E C O W M U N V U W
C S C D E A F E E Y E P A
U A N D W M N L S Z C G R
O M E A N S A K M S E E Y
T J I E Y T K E E D T G E
E L C N E W N A M P R N V
L L I K S T O C E E O E R
O T F O Q H W O N I F I E
S E O Q H G H E S W A S W
L O R H L I O U C L I N O
E K P A R M W E F E R A P
```

- CLEVERNESS
- ENERGY
- FLAIR
- FORCE
- FORTE
- GENIUS
- KNACK
- KNOW-HOW
- MASTERY
- MEANS
- MIGHT
- POWER
- PROFICIENCY
- PROWESS
- SCOPE
- SKILL
- TALENT
- TOUCH

20 Timber

```
E L A G N I B U B E L C P
S A P E L E I D H U O E I
G B L C E D A R E O C A V
U P R E S A N S B B P L R
C H E R R Y T M E C O Y A
Y N A G O H A M D H G N B
W V A V T B L H E C E T Y
H E W J U M D C L R E N B
I S C O N A E E A I S A B
T M A R L P R E U B L P H
E E I U A L O B E S T T R
O R J B W E I H A H E S T
A B T U L I P W O O D A Y
K A E S E N A P E N E H S
H U R E A N A R A P T A P
```

- ALDER
- BALSA
- BAMBOO
- BEECH
- BIRCH
- BUBINGA
- CEDAR
- CHERRY
- EBONY
- MAHOGANY
- MAPLE
- MERBAU
- PARANA
- SAPELE
- TULIPWOOD
- WALNUT
- WHITE OAK
- WILLOW

21 Architectural Details

```
E G F H A M B R I N O L E
L N I D Y L G E T V M O H
L Z N E Z E I R F S A M R
I T I Y E D L G T W D E S
R U A D K L N T W O N T R
G K L Z L I L E M D U N E
R E W O T I N R E N T A T
F I R U Z O R R Y I O I F
L C L R T A C U S W R H A
S F F S A B U T M E N T R
W Y P D E I A J Z G I N A
U A R C H W A Y I O N I C
C D L N I N T E R I Z R E
U J T L C A M P E L A O T
T U R T S D E R I S M C L
```

- ABUTMENT
- ARCHWAY
- CAPSTONE
- CORINTHIAN
- FINIAL
- FLUTING
- FRIEZE
- GRILLE
- IONIC
- RAFTERS
- RENDER
- ROTUNDA
- SCROLL
- STRUT
- TOWER
- TURRET
- WALLS
- WINDOWS

22 Bright

```
K R A T S F G V R C G Q L
L H H S R A H A I B U C U
T L P K R K P S R V Q L F
N G N I L K N I W T I I R
E Q S L U L L E C B G D E
C H F P R L W A S X T N E
S Y P T I A U E D H J G H
E U H A D M S S P C O I C
D Z N S S N R L T K N W Q
N T K N E I I A Q R O M Y
A N B T Y G L E E R O I Q
C K N E H E A V W L E U G
N I U T E P L A E N C E S
I D I C U L L E P R B P Y
W E D I D N E L P S Y E U
```

- BRILLIANT
- CHEERFUL
- CLEAR
- GARISH
- HARSH
- INCAN-DESCENT

- INTENSE
- LIGHT
- LURID
- LUSTROUS
- PELLUCID
- SHOWY

- SILVERY
- SPLENDID
- STARK
- SUNNY
- TWINKLING
- VIVID

23 Toys and Playthings

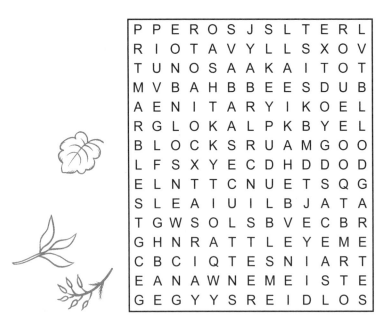

```
P P E R O S J S L T E R L
R I O T A V Y L L S X O V
T U N O S A A K A I T O T
M V B A H B B E E S D U B
A E N I T A R Y I K O E L
R G L O K A L P K B Y E L
B L O C K S R U A M G O O
L F S X Y E C D H D D O D
E L N T T C N U E T S Q G
S L E A I U I L B J A T A
T G W S O L S B V E C B R
G H N R A T T L E Y E M E
C B C I Q T E S N I A R T
E A N A W N E M E I S T E
G E G Y Y S R E I D L O S
```

- BICYCLE
- BLOCKS
- FOOTBALL
- HULA HOOP
- MARBLES
- PINATA

- RAG DOLL
- RATTLE
- ROUNDABOUT
- RUBIK'S CUBE
- SLEDGE
- SLIDE

- SOLDIERS
- STILTS
- SWING
- TRAIN SET
- WATER PISTOL
- YACHT

24 Archery

```
V F O O T E D A R R O W R
E L C U S R W G C R E E P
N I A O I E N E K L L T V
E G F F V I A L I E L A E
M H T D K E O P A F R L C
A T K C A Y R S Y O H P N
H S A K E M E S U I Y S S
C T T M E G B N T M P E A
S L A L A K D I A R E W W
A U P P E R L I M B U T E
R O P A B L Y T U B A N B
A P P S E O D L R V A R G
H E G R H R A A I N A E Q
Y L L E B O B M K R E N T
T N S I R E T N I F U Y E
```

- ASCHAM
- BARB
- BELLY
- CREEP
- DRIFT
- FLIGHT
- FOOTED ARROW
- OVERSTRUNG
- PILE
- PLATE
- RELEASE
- ROUND
- STACKING
- TILLER
- UPPER LIMB
- UPSHOT
- VANE
- YEW

25 Nursery Words

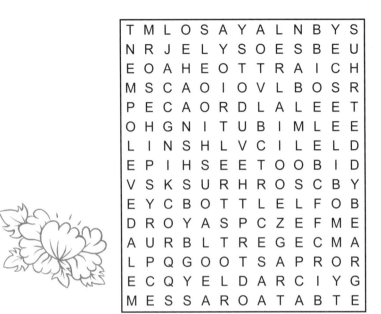

```
T M L O S A Y A L N B Y S
N R J E L Y S O E S B E U
E O A H E O T T R A I C H
M S C A O I O V L B O S R
P E C A O R D L A L E E T
O H G N I T U B I M L E E
L I N S H L V C I L E L D
E P I H S E E T O O B I D
V S K S U R H R O S C B Y
E Y C B O T T L E L F O B
D R O Y A S P C Z E F M E
A U R B L T R E G E C M A
L P Q G O O T S A P R O R
E C Q Y E L D A R C I Y G
M E S S A R O A T A B T E
```

- BABIES
- BATHTIME
- BOOTEES
- BOTTLE
- COLIC
- CRADLE
- CRIB
- DEVELOPMENT
- LOTION
- LULLABY
- MOBILE
- ROCKING
- ROSEHIP SYRUP
- RUSKS
- SLEEP
- STROLLER
- TEDDY BEAR
- TOYS

26 Circus

```
T D S T S R L Y S A W E L
T P P E S R E D S R U P H
I R S C C L E N C R F O I
F E A B H S E D O L O R T
N T G M L I S H I P T T P
A S E A P G L V S R C H A
O I L I N O R D S B S G P
U T O I R N L L R A A I S
S R R T T E L I C E V T K
M A T R Y I G R N P N S C
D E E N R F O A O E E N I
O A N H F B I N N F E W R
T U T F A T I F H E T O T
F C S T C E L A S W M L T
L A S E S A V N A C E C E
```

- ACROBATS
- ARTISTE
- CANVAS
- CHILDREN
- CLOWNS
- DARING
- FUNNY
- GASPS
- HOOPS
- MENAGERIE
- PONIES
- RIDERS
- TENTS
- THRILLS
- TIGHTROPE
- TRAMPOLINE
- TREAT
- TRICKS

27 Garden Pond

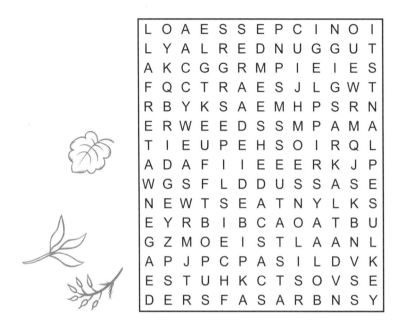

```
L O A E S S E P C I N O I
L Y A L R E D N U G G U T
A K C G G R M P I E I E S
F Q C T R A E S J L G W T
R B Y K S A E M H P S R N
E R W E E D S S M P A M A
T I E U P E H S O I R Q L
A D A F I I E E R K J P
W G S F L D D U S S A S E
N E W T S E A T N Y L K S
E Y R B I B C A O A T B U
G Z M O E I S T L A A N L
A P J P C P A S I L D V K
E S T U H K C T S O V S E
D E R S F A S A R B N S Y
```

- ALGAE
- BRIDGE
- CASCADE
- DESIGN
- GRASSES
- NEWTS
- NYMPH
- PLANTS
- REFLECTION
- RIPPLE
- ROCKS
- SKIMMER
- SLABS
- STATUES
- TOADS
- UNDERLAY
- WATERFALL
- WEEDS

28 Things with Buttons

```
M H R E N J H P E L E T D
A V O A F A L B O X R O P
D L T P M C G U F I Z A L
A L A H A K E I H S O R R
P D L R C E M S D A X E E
L U U L M T R T U R H M T
O N C X E C A A E O A A S
R G L B O K L W S A L C I
T A A L B B A O P I U B G
N R C E O V E R C O A T E
O E A N U B R K A K T Z R
C E Y D S F I P U O J S H
T S E E I F F A M J A S S
A R I R J O Y S T I C K A
A V L L E B R O O D E R C
```

- ALARM CLOCK
- BLENDER
- BLOUSE
- CALCULATOR
- CAMERA
- CARDIGAN

- CASH REGISTER
- CONTROL PAD
- DOORBELL
- DUNGAREES
- FIRE ALARM
- JACKET

- JOYSTICK
- JUKEBOX
- OVERCOAT
- RADIO
- SHIRT
- STOPWATCH

Maybe that's what life
is... a wink of the eye
and winking stars.

Jack Kerouac

29 Sauces

```
E T I H W P R O T S E P A
S E A R E E M V G E S N O
V I N A I G R E T T E T A
A N T D A C T U U I A S T
R E I R H A O N R M O A Y
E C L E R L S I O U M Y N
D I E T E O P T B M R A C
C S A V H I K I E R E R A
E R A E R D S E U B U L P
E S F I R E N C K A T S E
R E P P E P S C S C H E R
A C R E M E A N G L A I S
E R I O G L T O C I R P A
T S Y L B O P P R E P A S
A Y E L S R A P S E E T S
```

- APRICOT
- BLACK BEAN
- CAPER
- CHEESE
- CREME ANGLAIS
- CURRY
- GARLIC
- LEMON
- PARSLEY
- PEPPER
- PESTO
- PIRI-PIRI
- SOUBISE
- TARTARE
- TOMATO
- VELOUTE
- VINAIGRETTE
- WHITE

30　Pizza

```
W A S I E S E V I L O R E
G R O U N D B E E F O N G
T R E O O N C N O L B T A
F E I U C A G O I T U M S
M N G W P E N S O N G M U
O H D E W A S P A A J U A
Z W R I G V P E R A E S S
Z S R E U I X L E A S H N
A R R D N Q I S F H R R G
R O J G E C S P B N C O N
E P S S K S T I O O A O A
L C E U C F Z C B U U M F
L U T U I M A Y K R E S F
A H B K H B R I S E N A D
O G C E C U A S Q B B E R
```

- BACON
- BBQ SAUCE
- CAPERS
- CHEESE
- CHICKEN
- DOUGH

- GARLIC
- GROUND BEEF
- MOZZARELLA
- MUSHROOMS
- OLIVES
- ONIONS

- OREGANO
- SAUSAGE
- SPICY
- SQUID
- TOPPINGS
- TUNA

31 Made of Paper

```
N L I K I S T A W E L M D
M E C L T R O W E A W A S
A A W U J O V I B M D E M
S M E S N X W E X A G K D
A P N R L E L E P A P R Q
M E A T F E M E L A A E Y
P R L D U S T L Y C X C Q
A A P N B O O T T M E I N
M D D E N C Z S E V N O A
D N Y R T O O G P R P V V
A E O S Y P G E R U B N E
O L D I R E C T O R Y I L
R A C H A I N C D I A R Y
N C C N I K P A N O I H R
A P K O O B E N O H P E B
```

- CALENDAR
- CHAIN
- COLLAGE
- COUPON
- DIARY
- DIRECTORY
- INVOICE
- LABEL
- MENU
- NAPKIN
- NEWSLETTER
- NOTEPAD
- PHONE BOOK
- PLANE
- POSTCARD
- ROADMAP
- SACK
- TOWEL

32　Cocktails

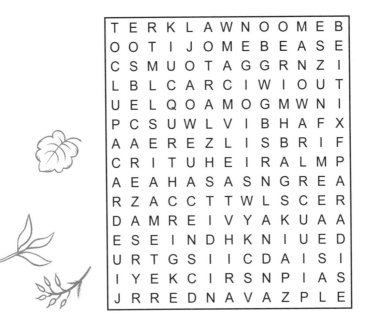

```
T E R K L A W N O O M E B
O O T I J O M E B E A S E
C S M U O T A G G R N Z I
L B L C A R C I W I O U T
U E L Q O A M O G M W N I
P C S U W L V I B H A F X
A A E R E Z L I S B R I F
C R I T U H E I R A L M P
A E A H A S A S N G R E A
R Z A C C T T W L S C E R
D A M R E I V Y A K U A A
E S E I N D H K N I U E D
U R T G S I I C D A I S I
I Y E K C I R S N P I A S
J R R E D N A V A Z P L E
```

- ACAPULCO
- BLUE HAWAII
- BRONX
- CHI-CHI
- COBBLER
- GIMLET
- JULEP
- MAN-O'-WAR
- MOJITO
- MOONWALK
- PARADISE
- RICKEY
- RUSTY NAIL
- SAZERAC
- SIDECAR
- STINGER
- TOM COLLINS
- ZOMBIE

33 Setting a Table

```
N H A P N A S U S Y Z A L
E F L O W E R S T S D N A
E A U T V U S A K E A G R
R Y T I L T O R M P R V A
U L N A P B O Z K J U I N
T K D K Y F D I O R B N R
P L P V K E N P E P P E R
E L A P W A T E R J U G E
A R A C L E M D A R J A A
G N F C V A M U S T A R D
D E S S E R T S P O O N A
S S A O D M H E G H O H E
E A G T J N A N S O R C R
A L L W O B T I U R F B
M E G T R E A D F R A W C
```

- BREAD
- DESSERT SPOON
- FLOWERS
- FORKS
- FRUIT BOWL
- GRAVY BOAT
- KNIVES
- LADLE
- LAZY SUSAN
- MUSTARD
- NAPKIN
- PEPPER
- PLACE MAT
- PLATES
- SALT
- TUREEN
- VINEGAR
- WATER JUG

34 Stitches

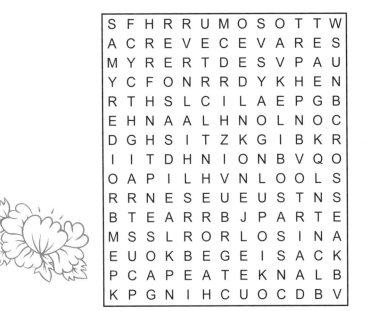

```
S F H R R U M O S O T T W
A C R E V E C E V A R E S
M Y R E R T D E S V P A U
Y C F O N R R D Y K H E N
R T H S L C I L A E P G B
E H N A A L H N O L N O C
D G H S I T Z K G I B K R
I I T D H N I O N B V Q O
O A P I L H V N L O O L S
R R N E S E U E U S T N S
B T E A R R B J P A R T E
M S S L R O R L O S I N A
E U O K B E G E I S A C K
P C A P E A T E K N A L B
K P G N I H C U O C D B V
```

- BLANKET
- BLIND
- BOBBLE
- CABLE
- CHAIN
- COUCHING
- CROSS
- EMBROIDERY
- FRENCH KNOT
- HERRINGBONE
- LADDER
- OVERCAST
- OVERLOCK
- RUNNING
- SASHIKO
- SATIN
- SCROLL
- STRAIGHT

35 Cleaning

```
R N E E R I S T R O R A T
X A W S E E B A M E W M A
A T O M T S G W Z S I O W
W E M P Z N H N P O P O N
E T D A E I B O O T E R E
R C N M T R M E A P S B H
Q W I E E D F O A M S L S
C R N H G Y A N H N T C E
G E T S H R E L E S R Q R
R A X T O W E L B U U V F
L C N M S G D T B E O R C
E R O P E N U B E I R L B
S K R A A L I V C D O R E
A A P K C N E O B T V Z M
Y O A K G S T A H A Z E I
```

- APRON
- BEESWAX
- BROOM
- BRUSH
- CLOTH
- DETERGENT
- FOAM
- FRESHEN
- GRIME
- LATHER
- MOPS
- RINSE
- SCRUBBING
- SPONGE
- SPRAY
- TOWEL
- WHITENER
- WIPES

36 Vegetables

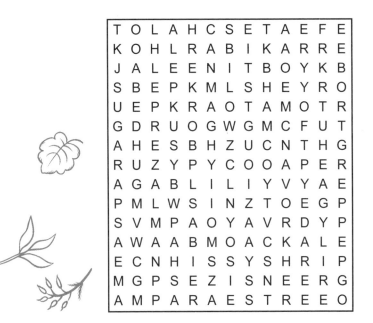

```
T O L A H C S E T A E F E
K O H L R A B I K A R R E
J A L E E N I T B O Y K B
S B E P K M L S H E Y R O
U E P K R A O T A M O T R
G D R U O G W G M C F U T
A H E S B H Z U C N T H G
R U Z Y P Y C O O A P E R
A G A B L I L I Y V Y A E
P M L W S I N Z T O E G P
S V M P A O Y A V R D Y P
A W A A B M O A C K A L E
E C N H I S S Y S H R I P
M G P S E Z I S N E E R G
A M P A R A E S T R E E O
```

- ARTICHOKE
- ASPARAGUS
- BROCCOLI
- CAPSICUM
- ESCHALOT
- GOURD
- GREENS
- KALE
- KOHLRABI
- MAIZE
- OKRA
- ONION
- PEAS
- PEPPER
- SAVOY
- SPINACH
- TOMATO
- YAM

37 Paper Types

```
S A I S E N A R D S E Y P
T O G E N A U F R E W R T
W H I T E W A T E D X E N
I E L L I N E N C V K A N
B A V N O S W A Y P F T W
P G V B F M S H C I G B O
A A R L R D Y U L R U Z R
R A P K T W S T E D R I B
C V L Y W O E E D I U H B
H X Y A R R N B I B F S Y
M D L Q M U H R A R R A A
E L R M M U S I C K F W V
N P E N J E P E R C I R C
T L L L A G E L Z F S N F
L A M T E Y G A L M R Y G
```

- BAKING
- BROWN
- CARBON
- CREPE
- FILTER
- GREEN

- LEGAL
- LINEN
- MUSIC
- NEWS
- PAPYRUS
- PARCHMENT

- RECYCLED
- TISSUE
- WALL
- WASHI
- WAXED
- WHITE

38 Hotel

```
Y R A R B I L M Y W R R P
N A P P G R O I A K E E O
G E G R E O B I D K T T S
W U F Y R P T L R H S R L
S E O D M E O G E S I O H
B R E I R N O F E A G P E
A B W K S E A W T E E G A
B K N G E I V S M N R M P
L E E M A N U R I S Y S R
E G O Y L O D G E U Y I E
A N U A S P J B B I M R R
G U E S T S P F R T M U A
E O R V N E N I L E W O W
K L A E L A V I R R A T S
I E G R E I C N O C O K H
```

- ARRIVAL
- BEDROOM
- CONCIERGE
- EN SUITE
- GUESTS
- GYMNASIUM

- KEYS
- LIBRARY
- LINEN
- LODGE
- LOUNGE
- PORTER

- REGISTER
- SAUNA
- STAIRS
- TOURISM
- WAITER
- WEEKEND BREAK

39 Coins

```
S Y N N E P E R K Y P A R
T H O D O C P F L O R I N
A V O S E S T E R C E D A
C M L R S W P L I D E E R
K D B E E O D E A O Y N Y
L L U Q U D A F J L D A C
E W O N R I L A K L Q R R
K M D U E G Q I F A S I Q
I I K R P B P I E G A S D
N D A Y O P E L L E T D U
T O V N C A A Z L L L L C
F R B Y G H T A A U I H A
U E P L T E F E H N G H T
S E N R E B L A V S T S S
```

- ANGEL
- BEZANT
- COPPER
- DENARIUS
- DOLLAR
- DOUBLOON

- DUCAT
- FLORIN
- GROAT
- GUILDER
- MOIDORE
- NICKEL

- NOBLE
- PENNY
- POUND
- SESTERCE
- SHILLING
- THALER

40 Robin Hood

```
E N E E R G N L O C N I L
H T Y M E P E V D R U C P
F L E W O T S N I W D E N
H O J Y T R E V O P A P E
L D R H Y G R U E R I S D
O A T E E T T A C M J T A
X L L L S A I H E T D H E
L L D A X T E R K P E G A
E A R E T R R J A L D I B
Y B S R Y Y T O E H S N E
Z U S O M D E A M D C K H
H S G E U B U C R A G B P
I U N R L A W O B G N O L
B J A G I P W D Z K E C Y
A R E L T S A F J O P T E
```

- ARCHERY
- BALLAD
- CHARITY
- EDWINSTOWE
- FOREST
- KNIGHTS
- LEGEND
- LINCOLN GREEN
- LONGBOW
- LOXLEY
- MERRY MEN
- MYTH
- POVERTY
- ROMANCE
- SIR GUY
- SWORDS
- TARGET
- TAXES

41 Stormy Weather

```
D E Q U A L L T S A M E R
S U O U T S E P M E T P A
T Y L Z O D S B B Y L T I
R H D L E D B Q D L F A V
I O U L N R A N U C O E G
U N U N P E I N L A L W H
T G C G D W S O R Z L W Y
E V T L H E U S Z O C L Y
R S S O E D R I I S T V Y
A R A Q B M R Y G Q A Z M
M P C U E D E W C E U I O
U L R E S A B N H I V E O
A S E I H E V H T V K R L
T L V A W M I S T Y E A G
A R O G N I G A R I N G Y
```

- BLOWY
- CLOUDBURST
- DELUGE
- DRIZZLE
- DULLNESS
- GALES
- GLOOMY
- HEAVY
- INCLEMENT
- MISTY
- OVERCAST
- RAGING
- ROUGH
- SQUALLY
- TEMPESTUOUS
- THUNDERY
- TORNADO
- WINDY

To have faith is to trust yourself to the water. When you swim you don't grab hold of the water, because if you do you will sink and drown. Instead you relax, and float.

Alan Watts

42 Greece

```
A A B E G O I I U B R S E
N T L A O F A K P A T C U
I R A I Y A A L A R A I S
S A B P D E A S O R C U N
T P C M H K A I H H E F E
E S C Y A R Y T Z Z D R S
R C S L E R O G U A E O E
E C S O Z G R D O T J C N
S O X A N S A W I O R N N
R H O D E S G D A T U T O
E F A V M G T N T U E Z P
D O I S G F E T H D U S O
S L K A R I O A E V E C L
O S A N T O R I N I C R E
A K I N O L A S S Y E S P
```

- AEGEAN
- APHRODITE
- ATHENS
- CORFU
- NAXOS
- OLIVES

- OLYMPIA
- OUZO
- PELOPONNESE
- PLAKA
- RAKI
- RETSINA

- RHODES
- SALONIKA
- SANTORINI
- SPARTA
- THRACE
- ZEUS

43 Furnishings

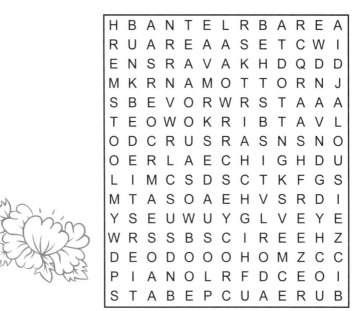

```
H B A N T E L R B A R E A
R U A R E A A S E T C W I
E N S R A V A K H D Q D D
M K R N A M O T T O R N J
S B E V O R W R S T A A A
T E O W O K R I B T A V L
O D C R U S R A S N S N O
O E R L A E C H I G H D U
L I M C S D S C T K F G S
M T A S O A E H V S R D I
Y S E U W U Y G L V E Y E
W R S S B S C I R E E H Z
D E O D O O O H O M Z C C
P I A N O L R F D C E O I
S T A B E P C U A E R U B
```

- BUNK BED
- BUREAU
- CHEST
- CLOSET
- COUCH
- DESK
- DRESSER
- FREEZER
- HIGH CHAIR
- JALOUSIE
- LARDER
- MIRROR
- OTTOMAN
- OVEN
- PIANO
- SOFA
- STOOL
- WASHSTAND

44   US States

```
A  I  N  R  O  F  I  L  A  C  R  I  M
I  I  A  W  A  H  A  L  A  S  K  A  I
A  D  I  R  O  L  F  B  A  H  V  Q  C
R  E  P  L  O  U  I  S  I  A  N  A  H
I  M  I  C  H  E  N  A  E  S  Z  W  I
Z  E  O  J  K  A  S  A  R  I  K  F  G
O  W  K  E  K  A  I  G  R  O  E  G  A
N  E  L  R  E  Z  N  N  V  N  N  W  N
A  R  A  V  P  S  B  O  E  I  T  Y  I
U  E  H  E  E  B  S  G  O  L  U  O  N
T  A  O  R  M  R  S  E  I  L  C  M  I
E  S  M  A  L  A  M  R  N  I  K  I  A
A  F  A  S  D  O  I  O  U  N  Y  N  A
A  D  A  V  E  N  A  N  N  B  E  G  N
T  V  D  Y  T  W  E  A  E  T  J  T  E
```

- ALASKA
- ARIZONA
- ARKANSAS
- CALIFORNIA
- FLORIDA
- GEORGIA

- HAWAII
- ILLINOIS
- KENTUCKY
- LOUISIANA
- MAINE
- MICHIGAN

- NEVADA
- OKLAHOMA
- OREGON
- TENNESSEE
- VERMONT
- WYOMING

45 Collectibles

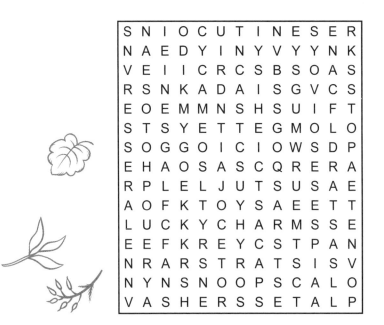

```
S N I O C U T I N E S E R
N A E D Y I N Y V Y Y N K
V E I I C R C S B S O A S
R S N K A D A I S G V C S
E O E M M N S H S U I F T
S T S Y E T T E G M O L O
S O G G O I C I O W S D P
E H A O S A S C Q R E R A
R P L E L J U T S U S A E
A O F K T O Y S A E E T T
L U C K Y C H A R M S S E
E E F K R E Y C S T P A N
N R A R S T R A T S I S V
N Y N S N O O P S C A L O
V A S H E R S S E T A L P
```

- ANTIQUES

- CAMEOS

- COINS

- COMICS

- FANS

- FLAGS

- LUCKY CHARMS

- MUGS

- NECKLACES

- PHOTOS

- PLATES

- ROCKS

- SPOONS

- STAMPS

- TEAPOTS

- TICKETS

- TOYS

- VASES

46 Fabrics

```
N Y M E R I N O D U E S Z
D R K Z O M N L H K Z I A
I U D U Y H N O T T O C R
A Y N A T O L E F N O R A
L T M G M S C W C F O H D
P A N K A A O I W U I S Z
Q R S V R R S I L L A H C
I T N T V H E K L A Y I C
J A A U R R E U S C I C
C N A F I A E I R E K C F
H B R O F N K N C Z N I E
W G M Q B E J H I Y K I N
E S U R P P T D A M Y I E
A J R U A Z R A H N R V D
P P E R E K C U S R E E S
```

- ARMURE
- ASTRAKHAN
- CALICO
- CANVAS
- CHALLIS
- CHIFFON
- COTTON
- DAMASK
- DUNGAREE
- ERMINE
- GAUZE
- MERINO
- MOIRE
- OILSKIN
- PLAID
- SEERSUCKER
- TAFFETA
- TARTAN

47 Garden Creatures

G	I	N	E	F	L	E	S	T	E	R	T	E
U	R	E	D	A	N	T	G	T	W	R	T	S
L	O	D	E	M	X	G	A	I	E	E	E	U
S	B	H	Y	R	S	R	Y	B	A	P	K	O
H	I	C	E	U	E	P	E	B	N	P	C	M
O	N	G	O	D	G	F	A	A	E	O	I	W
R	O	I	H	Y	G	R	Y	R	S	H	R	G
N	E	L	T	E	S	E	P	M	R	G	C	A
E	G	N	C	P	U	E	H	D	V	O	H	L
T	I	M	I	U	A	M	R	O	G	R	W	L
S	P	D	A	M	K	P	E	Z	G	F	I	F
A	E	V	O	H	F	D	A	R	N	A	U	L
R	A	T	M	A	U	A	B	U	N	E	B	Y
K	H	E	R	U	A	J	E	S	H	R	E	W
A	S	E	D	E	P	I	L	L	I	M	E	N

- CRICKET
- FROG-HOPPER
- GALLFLY
- HEDGEHOG
- HORNET
- LEAF MINER

- MILLIPEDE
- MOUSE
- PEA MOTH
- PIGEON
- RABBIT
- RED ANT

- ROBIN
- SHREW
- SLUG
- SNAIL
- SPARROW
- SPIDER

48 Ball Games

```
T P E R A S P E R W O N B
B O U L E S E M G S F I E
P L L A B E L N K H R Y S
T E H U N C O B V I H L C
P B T P E P T Y B N F N R
I A A A G H A O D T V U H
B G D N N D L A F Y G S E
K A I D D Q B V N B R D S
S P G U L Y U D Y E J R S
A C S A P E J E D A S A O
M E U M T E B N I K Q I R
A R O C C E U A E H U L C
L E A C M O L M L E A L A
U F O A R A X L F L S I L
G B W M I N I T E N H B Z
```

- BAGATELLE
- BANDY
- BILLIARDS
- BIRIBOL
- BOCCE
- BOULES

- JAI ALAI
- LACROSSE
- MINITEN
- PADDLE BALL
- PELOTA
- PETANQUE

- PING-PONG
- ROUNDERS
- RUGBY
- SHINTY
- SQUASH
- ULAMA

49 Aromatherapy

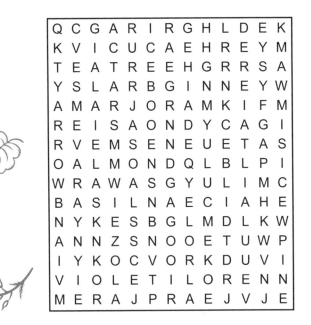

```
Q C G A R I R G H L D E K
K V I C U C A E H R E Y M
T E A T R E E H G R R S A
Y S L A R B G I N N E Y W
A M A R J O R A M K I F M
R E I S A O N D Y C A G I
R V E M S E N E U E T A S
O A L M O N D Q L B L P I
W R A W A S G Y U L I M C
B A S I L N A E C I A H E
N Y K E S B G L M D L K W
A N N Z S N O O E T U W P
I Y K O C V O R K D U V I
V I O L E T I L O R E N N
M E R A J P R A E J V J E
```

- ALMOND
- BASIL
- BAY LEAF
- CITRONELLA
- CLOVE
- GINGER
- JONQUIL
- MANGO
- MARJORAM
- MIMOSA
- MYRRH
- NEROLI
- NUTMEG
- PEONY
- PINE
- TEA TREE
- VIOLET
- YARROW

50 Wind and Brass Instruments

```
A C I D O L E M O C E R T
N O O S S A B R E D I S E
O O Z A R T E P M U R T L
S R E R V D A K M E S Z O
B H A V R H O V A O Z B E
T M A O U H Y L U Z E Q G
H C C W H N A S O T O R A
O E R T M A A U E C M O L
R S N P E P R T T J C R F
N T X A H N U M S B T I O
P V U O O L I J O T O E P
I I N B F B I R W N Z Y F
P E R D A I O K A A I C W
E A H C I B F E E L R C B
I C E L G U B E E A C I A
```

- BASSOON
- BUGLE
- CLARINET
- FIFE
- FLAGEOLET
- FLUTE

- HARMONICA
- HAUTBOY
- HORNPIPE
- KAZOO
- MELODICA
- OBOE

- PICCOLO
- RECORDER
- SHAWM
- SOUSAPHONE
- TRUMPET
- TUBA

51 Asteroids and Satellites

```
A A D A S S A L A H T E U
W A M E A Y G J E E T I S
M T I P P H M H A R P G E
T S I G P T N O R E B O M
A R D Y H E N A O N G L U
N B I M O T A K D C J S M
A O V T S K B E N E C I B
B O R A O I I K A L R A R
A O M A N N L A P A N R I
W I U R H D A S N D S N E
M H T F K C C D E U Q A L
Z X X R Y S A H N S F Q T
G C W Y O A E A K A M A N
Q I O S P P J K V I I Y H
K D X P S O M I E D M M T
```

- CALIBAN
- CHARON
- DEIMOS
- ENCELADUS
- HYDRA
- JANUS

- MIMAS
- MIRANDA
- NAMAKA
- OBERON
- PANDORA
- PORTIA

- SAPPHO
- SIARNAQ
- TETHYS
- THALASSA
- TRITON
- UMBRIEL

52 Nuts and Seeds

```
S L C E L E Y R E L E C A
A S U N F L O W E R C A M
W N M E R N S A A A L S Z
E L I Z A R B N R L J H P
M D N S D B V A E G N E N
A N W N E O W M H H P U D
S O I H C A T S I P B N T
E M P T Y R N C Q Y E A L
S L D U U N K N N E T C S
Y A A I M O F N A L E E M
E P T U R P T L Y T L R P
E M P Y A G K W Y B T E E
D A R O J C G I K J C O V
Y C E L P R O W N A N Q U
W E H S A C F E N N E L Q
```

- ALMOND
- ANISE
- ANNATTO
- BETEL
- BRAZIL
- CARAWAY

- CASHEW
- CELERY
- CUMIN
- FENNEL
- HICKORY
- PECAN

- PISTACHIO
- POPPY
- PUMPKIN
- SESAME
- SUNFLOWER
- WALNUT

53 Sailing

```
K A N O I T A G I V A N D
T V E R B C A Y H S A D E
A I L B I N N A C L E S F
O T S Y G M Y A H C T I A
L U C W R E S O H T R E B
F F A R L R J E T T I E S
R Y T L U Y O B E E I D N
E T A J H I M H G R F E Y
T G M D L J S A C O L Y A
A X A R F E Y I R N A O C
W W R R S O S E N R A C H
N J A N V A D S P G E S T
E H N G C E I S E H L D R
W Y G M C Y H L P V G S A
G I B K E M D E S O R E S
```

- ANCHOR
- BERTH
- BINNACLE
- CATAMARAN
- CRUISING
- FLOAT

- FOREDECK
- GALLEY
- GANGWAY
- JETTIES
- NAVIGATION
- SAILS

- SPRAY
- VESSEL
- VOYAGE
- WATER
- WHARF
- YACHT

54 Good-looking

```
G N I H C T E F Y R G D H
J U T S B A B D B O N N Y
W V J R D E N D Y S I A M
G R L C A A P I M E K R E
Y N Q O D M V G Y A A G M
B J I L V A S Y E D T P O
S E E R E E L V I J H E S
O A A D U E L A B V T M D
Y C D U P L N Y W U A O N
T N I A T T L G C C E S A
T I H U S I E A S O R N H
E S W Y E H F X O M B I E
R R H B A E I U K E D W T
P P E Y Y M A N L L E E E
R E P P A D E R G Y J A R
```

- ALLURING
- BEAUTIFUL
- BONNY
- BREATH-
  TAKING
- COMELY
- CUTE
- DANDY
- DAPPER
- DASHING
- FETCHING
- GRAND
- HANDSOME
- LOVELY
- PRETTY
- RADIANT
- SHAPELY
- SMART
- WINSOME

All of us have this
opportunity to find
true freedom, and
no one is exempt, no
one is disqualified,
because the light
of consciousness
burns in everyone.

Mooji

55 The Nordic Region

```
B N R U Y L C E S B E J D
R N E S O A O D D T T E V
E A P M Y K P G R A K D E
N T L G L E E O O N I N V
H S J E U O N G J V V A G
A A U D R D H F F I R L R
R L S P E N A R M X A T O
D M N L U L G N A M N U B
F A A Y A K E N A D S J I
I G N S S T N R I W D T V
S O P E O T I O E N S I O
K P L F C V E D R O R A R
U S O S E Y E R P W O E C
R L Q R O N O R W A A Y H
F J L A K E M J O S A Y R
```

- COPENHAGEN
- FJORDS
- GAMLA STAN
- GLAMA RIVER
- HARDFISKUR
- HERNING
- JUTLAND
- LAKE MJOSA
- LJUSNAN
- LOFOTEN
- NARVIK
- NORWAY
- OSLO
- RIDDAR-HOLMEN
- SWEDEN
- TRONDELAG
- UPPSALA
- VIBORG

56 Keep in Touch

```
L M M A N E S A C E V E K
I N T E R A C T M I A K C
A K E Y T T R A N S M I T
M T Y A P A E F N U A U E
R U L P X P O R E P O R T
I K I I S R T M Y Z E X A
A K A S M G X F E T C I C
K A I S O C I S I A O S I
A R S O H T R R L T T C N
E A E G O E W L H E T H U
P S W N V Y U E M X A A M
S I F N C P M D E T H N M
C L O D V E P M T T C G O
A C K N O W L E D G E D C
H U F R A N S E T O A T E
```

- ACKNOWL-
  EDGE

- AIRMAIL

- CALL UP

- CHAT TO

- COMMUNI-
  CATE

- CONVERSE

- GOSSIP

- INFORM

- INTERACT

- LIAISE

- NOTIFY

- REPORT

- SPEAK

- TALK

- TEXT

- TRANSMIT

- TWEET

- WRITE

57 Backing Groups

```
S G N I W E T M I D A S L
A S N A D U E E S E W A B
M R S J E K B C E O I E N
R E L T Y B Y H D S P I P
U D L E E S U A P W V S P
M I G O E M H N A S E A S
O A H V D S O I N E Z L U
E R A L G Y L C H Y L I N
R W M S Y E M S D A M A I
G J A I R P N A B E O E O
B N C S S A K E K X N X N
L V A W B O R E E E M Y G
E S E G T I R A S M R C A
T N N A F H E R M I T S P
S F S E O N I M O D E S B
```

- BANSHEES
- BUNNYMEN
- COMETS
- DAKOTAS
- DOMINOES
- FIREBALLS

- GANG
- HERMITS
- MECHANICS
- MELODY MAKERS
- NEWS
- PIPS

- RAIDERS
- SHADOWS
- UNION GAP
- WAILERS
- WAVES
- WINGS

58 Yellow Things

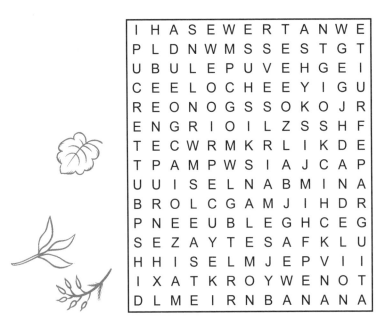

```
I H A S E W E R T A N W E
P L D N W M S S E S T G T
U B U L E P U V E H G E I
C E E L O C H E E Y I G U
R E O N O G S S O K O J R
E N G R I O I L Z S S H F
T E C W R M K R L I K D E
T P A M P W S I A J C A P
U U I S E L N A B M I N A
B R O L C G A M J I H D R
P N E E U B L E G H C E G
S E Z A Y T E S A F K L U
H H I S E L M J E P V I I
I X A T K R O Y W E N O T
D L M E I R N B A N A N A
```

- BANANA
- BUTTERCUP
- CHICKS
- CROCUS
- DANDELION
- EGG YOLK

- GOSLING
- GRAPEFRUIT
- JASMINE
- LEMON
- MAIZE
- MARIGOLD

- MELON
- NEW YORK TAXI
- PRIMROSE
- SPONGE
- THE SIMPSONS
- TULIP

59 Pantry Contents

```
S E M Y H T F O T Q P Q R
R E S A P R I N P R U U J
O E B A R Y C A A R O R A
L T D U F J D G S L S A S
F B T N C F O E F S E G S
E A C V A N R R I R M E E
E L T E G I O O A O B N V
R H E R B S R L N M Y I A
E G A P E R L O L R J V E
P R E S H R E I C I S A L
P A L A C S S A T E U T Y
E U V P R U N E S N D O A
P A R E G N I G S R E A B
H E S A D R U D K E R L S
N A R Y A E E F F O C A P
```

- BAY LEAVES
- BOUILLON CUBES
- COFFEE
- CORIANDER
- FLOUR
- GINGER

- HERBS
- LENTILS
- MARJORAM
- OREGANO
- PEPPER
- PRUNES

- PULSES
- SAFFRON
- SOUP
- SUGAR
- THYME
- VINEGAR

60 Schooldays

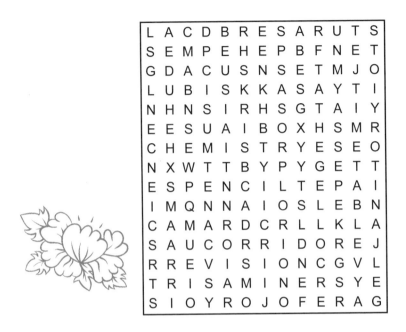

```
L A C D B R E S A R U T S
S E M P E H E P B F N E T
G D A C U S N S E T M J O
L U B I S K K A S A Y T I
N H N S I R H S G T A I Y
E E S U A I B O X H S M R
C H E M I S T R Y E S E O
N X W T T B Y P Y G E T T
E S P E N C I L T E P A I
I M Q N N A I O S L E B N
C A M A R D C R L L K L A
S A U C O R R I D O R E J
R R E V I S I O N C G V L
T R I S A M I N E R S Y E
S I O Y R O J O F E R A G
```

- BIOLOGY
- CANTEEN
- CHEMISTRY
- COLLEGE
- CORRIDOR
- DESKS

- DRAMA
- ESSAY
- GAMES
- JANITOR
- MARKS
- MUSIC

- PENCIL
- REVISION
- SCIENCE
- TESTS
- TIMETABLE
- TRUANCY

61 Indian Towns and Cities

```
J A C A A G R U P Z E T S
F R E N U K O L L A M E L
I K T N I R Z A R B C N L
M A T T D E P E R E S A F
P U E I V O Y G J A H M R
R Y Z H H P N H R P O R Y
C H R B L O A H M E V I E
B V U I L N T I H A T T S
N E R L S A Y A J Y Y S A
L A I I H Y D E R A B A D
C H M P G X S U R U T R P
S F C A Y I H L E D S N E
Z A N R D K U O A H N E M
T B A N G A L O R E N U P
D A G E E T L O O N R U K
```

- AMRITSAR
- BANGALORE
- BHOPAL
- DAMAN
- DELHI
- GUNTUR
- HATHRAS
- HYDERABAD
- IMPHAL
- JHANSI
- KOLLAM
- KURNOOL
- PATNA
- PILIBHIT
- PUNE
- SHILLONG
- SURAT
- TEZPUR

62 Collection

```
G A B D E X I M X I C A R
S I M I S H M A S H Y C E
A H F O G K C S O Y E C R
R T O R G K I I A V D U M
S L O T H A C N T M P M T
G U J O C E R O D N P U E
P A A V J H L R O S K L R
R R T T E B P P A C C A E
D M Y H O R B O A F O T S
U S E J E N A P T T E I E
U S F D R R M E S C A O G
K A R I L E I M T T H N N
C L U S T E R N J Y H C A
K C W A D B Y G G K R H R
H A Y T E I R A V E S E L
```

- ACCU-
  MULATION

- CHOICE

- CLASS

- CLUSTER

- FARRAGO

- GATHERING

- GROUP

- HOARD

- HOTCHPOTCH

- JOB-LOT

- KINDS

- MEDLEY

- MISHMASH

- MIXED BAG

- PACK

- RANGE

- SAMPLE

- VARIETY

63 Intelligence

```
P P N C A P A L T N Z G U
C U D O U C E S H I D N S
O L N E I A R R G C E I H
A V C R R T E V I H D W O
S A Y V E O A C S B A O G
T C B T F V T N N R E N E
U U H R I H E U I I H K N
T M L O G C Y L T G R I I
E E M U O N A W C H A L U
S N O O I L M G E T E M S
L H B A D J E E A K L M I
T W R U S S Y D N S C P V
O B T E E Q I C A T I S I
E R A A W A N W P R A H S
A H S S J D F A E S S L G
```

- ACUMEN
- ASTUTE
- BRAINY
- BRIGHT
- CLEAR-HEADED
- CLEVER
- GENIUS
- IMAGINATION
- INSIGHT
- KNOWING
- MENTAL
- SAGACITY
- SCHOOLED
- SHARP
- SHREWD
- THOUGHT
- TUTORED
- WISDOM

64 Cycling

```
E T T O R E N A N E Y H S
E L E H G R E A R S L L Q
R O C K S T W K I A A C R
G A V Y S J O H E D L N E
P T A G C A U E E S F I T
U A Z E S I B P C E T A E
M U D G U A R D V L L H M
P R Y G S K E T D B I C O
L I G H T S E L O E L P D
A S Z L E B D L C E C F E
E C O A S F T U E Y A Q E
Z C E R N S C M Y U C V P
K G A R S U A S W O L I S
A E D H V R T B G A A W B
G R A U F G S S V E R A Q
```

- BASKET
- BICYCLE
- BOLTS
- CHAIN
- COGS
- FRAME

- GEARS
- LIGHTS
- LOCK
- MUDGUARD
- NUTS
- PEDALS

- PUMP
- SPEEDOMETER
- TOE CLIP
- TRICYCLE
- VALVE
- WHEEL

65 Hairstyles

```
A G F R U S C U I P U T E
F O T O N S U R E L A E L
A F M M B E R B S A A I P
R F I R Y F L P E I A O O
I F A U U F E P Y T R V M
M I B F Q U D D Y F M P P
D U D U U O E N A P A Y A
O E L A K P O J H O R P D
M G J L M P Z S U R C A O
A D T I E O U S V C E G U
N J R L P T F A S H L E R
V C P Q U A F F N S W B H
T O P K N O T I N C A O U
D E B M O C K C A B V Y L
A E G B L S E V I H E E B
```

- AFRO
- BACK-COMBED
- BEEHIVE
- BRAID
- CRIMPED
- CROP
- CURLED
- MARCEL WAVE
- MULLET
- PAGEBOY
- PLAIT
- POMPADOUR
- PONYTAIL
- POUFFE
- QUIFF
- SKINHEAD
- TONSURE
- TOPKNOT

66 Cheeses

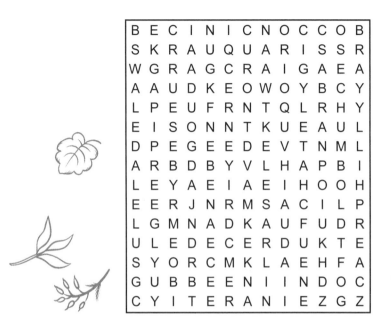

```
B E C I N I C N O C C O B
S K R A U Q U A R I S S R
W G R A G C R A I G A E A
A A U D K E O W O Y B C Y
L P E U F R N T Q L R H Y
E I S O N N T K U E A U L
D P E G E E D E V T N M L
A R B D B Y V L H A P B I
L E Y A E I A E I H O O H
E E R J N R M S A C I L P
L G M N A D K A U F U D R
U L E D E C E R D U K T E
S Y O R C M K L A E H F A
G U B B E E N I I N D O C
C Y I T E R A N I E Z G Z
```

- ALVERCA
- BANDEL
- BLUE VINNEY
- BOCCONCINI
- CAERPHILLY
- CERNEY
- DERBY
- DRY JACK
- EDAM
- GOUDA
- GRABETTO
- GUBBEEN
- HUMBOLDT FOG
- LEYDEN
- LIEDERKRANZ
- NEUFCHATEL
- QUARK
- SWALEDALE

67 Citrus Fruits

```
G Q C H U F R I U T E P K
R G M Z O L E M O P Z C H
A S U D A C H I U K O K E
P Y G A I E B R U D N M B
E J A L S B N S D E I E R
F E G A T A T A E L O D V
R U G V K A H A Y L D U T
U F D O N S A E Y A G A A
I F Y A R W K H E D N U U
T I M N O T M J A G O R Q
L A R N K E E L O R Z N M
L E N Z A N Z R N O A D U
T I M K A B O S U R D L K
K O R O B L A N C O E F S
C I P O N C I R U S H E R
```

- AMANATSU
- ETROG
- GRAPEFRUIT
- IYOKAN
- KABOSU
- KEY LIME

- KINNOW
- KUMQUAT
- LARAHA
- LEMON
- OROBLANCO
- POMELO

- PONCIRUS
- SHADDOCK
- SUDACHI
- TANGOR
- UGLI
- YUZU

Only that day dawns
to which we are
awake. There is more
day to dawn. The sun
is but a morning star.

Henry David Thoreau

68 Face

```
E C A M I R G E I C T E R
R E N I L R I A H E I L Y
E B C O M P L E X I O N S
F H O S S F E A C A I M Q
H K T S C K I G T F U J U
A M N U B O P P A S L E I
E E U O O Y W H C S Y N N
R L N F O M Y L N E I Q T
F E I Z A S E O L M A V H
H R C M L S S I H Z G U S
S G E A S T D O N W O R F
U O R C R S O M R Y A U T
L G K I K B I H G E A V A
B Z L S E L P M I D E R S
Z S O S D A E H E R O F E
```

- BLUSH
- CHEEKBONE
- COMPLEXION
- DIMPLES
- EARS
- EYELIDS

- FOREHEAD
- FRECKLE
- FROWN
- GRIMACE
- HAIR LINE
- MOUTH

- MUSCLES
- NOSTRILS
- SCOWL
- SMILE
- SQUINT
- VISAGE

69 Stage Plays

```
S G O O D E D R G O J Z E
U G E B F V Y R N E H A Y
E N V G Y N E S T N E G D
D S W E A T P M S D Y E B
A O K E M L E R U G V A N
M U O N S L I A U A V H S
A E H W P T A L Q M Z A H
E L R O Q V E Y E E L M V
O L N T N E V D A O G L A
M L U R D P U V M R D E S
A K S U T I R E B G T T A
O H A O A P C O B U P E R
H E L E N P J E O I R Y B
M J L B G I M A L F D I J
R I S U O N O L L E H T O
```

- *ADVENT*
- *AMADEUS*
- *BETRAYAL*
- *ENDGAME*
- *EQUUS*
- *GALILEO*

- *HAMLET*
- *HELEN*
- *HENRY V*
- *LE CID*
- *OSLO*
- *OTHELLO*

- *OUR TOWN*
- *PIPPIN*
- *PROOF*
- *SALOME*
- *SWEAT*
- *TANGO*

```
N F U E A A M R A P F C L
M L B S F C A M H A F E A
I O A E C P E S T A T B S
L R N G R A N S A S S O P
T E G T Z G S E E L F L E
U N A T E V A I P A T O Z
S C R P A C R M F Z O G I
C E B A O T E Y O I L N A
A G L C K Y D R S O E A N
N N O P O V N I V P A S C
Y O F E A R D E A I O P O
U C K I S N T S O U N F N
S C E L I V T I N E E O A
P H S R L A M E N H A L U
O I B P E R I T N A I H C
```

- ANCONA
- BERGAMO
- BOLOGNA
- BRINDISI
- CHIANTI
- CORTINA
- FLORENCE
- GNOCCHI
- GRAN SASSO
- LA SPEZIA
- LAZIO
- MONTE CERVINO
- NAPLES
- PARMA
- PASTA
- PIAVE
- TRIESTE
- TUSCANY

71 Things With Wings

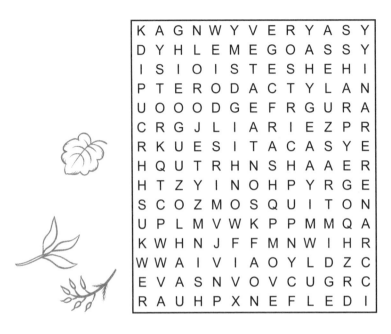

K A G N W Y V E R Y A S Y
D Y H L E M E G O A S S Y
I S I O I S T E S H E H I
P T E R O D A C T Y L A N
U O O O D G E F R G U R A
C R G J L I A R I E Z P R
R K U E S I T A C A S Y E
H Q U T R H N S H A A E R
H T Z Y I N O H P Y R G E
S C O Z M O S Q U I T O N
U P L M V W K P P M M Q A
K W H N J F F M N W I H R
W W A I V I A O Y L D Z C
E V A S N V O V C U G R C
R A U H P X N E F L E D I

- CRANE
- CUPID
- EAGLE
- FAIRY
- GLIDER
- GOOSE

- GRYPHON
- HARPY
- HAWK
- MIDGE
- MOSQUITO
- MOTH

- OSTRICH
- PTERODACTYL
- SPHINX
- STORK
- VAMPIRE
- WASP

72 Early

```
E C N S G V U O S L F W V
P A I A N A R E T A O E T
Y J L N U R E K J N R D S
T Y P V O U H A C I M A R
O P R H Y Y S E E G E U I
T R I O Q P R R V I R N F
O E O E T A R B Q R G R N
R V R C S C L Y M O E O K
P I E I U I U A O E O D L
A O Y T C G R D U S G L A
F U T U R E T N O R F N I
I S E W C I N O U R K P T
R H C T M H T G Y S T E I
E D N E A D V A N C E N N
T N E I P I C N I R A T I
```

- ADVANCE
- DAYBREAK
- EMBRYONIC
- FIRST
- FORMER
- FUTURE
- IN FRONT
- IN GOOD TIME
- INCIPIENT
- INITIAL
- INTRODUC-
  TORY
- ORIGINAL
- PREVIOUS
- PRIOR
- PROTOTYPE
- SUNRISE
- TOO SOON
- YOUNG

73 Sushi

```
I  Q  U  I  S  A  B  E  A  S  Y  A  M
B  A  R  C  M  G  D  P  P  E  G  B  A
A  I  K  U  R  A  P  W  L  S  A  B  R
S  S  Y  E  H  A  M  L  Y  A  T  K  I
A  L  A  O  K  J  O  Y  I  M  R  D  D
W  L  R  E  Y  W  E  H  O  E  A  O  I
M  O  E  S  T  S  S  P  S  Y  H  J
A  R  T  A  H  U  T  D  R  E  T  C  O
K  I  I  P  Z  O  S  E  K  E  O  O  M
I  L  C  E  R  H  G  E  R  D  F  P  A
M  Q  R  R  R  N  O  M  E  S  U  N  H
O  A  A  I  I  T  S  H  E  D  U  R  S
N  C  M  G  W  A  N  E  C  T  H  I  I
O  P  M  P  R  E  C  I  Y  O  T  C  A
W  A  S  I  M  E  Y  U  E  S  H  E  P
```

- CARROTS
- CRAB
- GINGER
- HOCHO
- IKURA
- KAPPA

- MAKIMONO
- NAREZUSHI
- OYSTERS
- RICE
- ROLLS
- SESAME SEEDS

- SHAMOJI
- SHRIMP
- TOFU
- TUNA
- WASABI
- YELLOWTAIL

74 The Chronicles of Narnia

```
K N R E A N A U A M G R T
I P R E R N E S T S P A A
N A V O A G U I D E L M R
G D N U M D E T T A W A U
T M S P L A A E E S I N N
I A L L E J R R A N N D A
R U A R T E M V R W S U P
I G M A K S H A A I J E E
A R I T I P N C Y M N S N
N I N V N E U H I T C V L
P M A R C U R E I P J A N
R R A B A D A S H J E A D
A H A N C S R P R E S E K
C A N E U O R D R U U P R
E F A S C R A H S E L B E
```

- ANIMALS
- ARAVIS
- ASLAN
- CHARN
- DARRIN
- EDMUND
- GUIDE
- KING TIRIAN
- MAUGRIM
- MAVRAMORN
- NARNIA
- PETER
- RABADASH
- RAMANDU
- REEPICHEEP
- SUSAN
- TELMAR
- TISROC

75 Novelists

```
I E L S L S F P G T B H V
D C W O Y L R F O Y A L R
H I H G N O R E F D G L P
M R E L U Y E L S G N I K
T P A S P L A I D Y O U L
B O T G L B R T N R L G E
I H L L N E G S O E D B T
I V E K T N S S A I B D N
E L Y R I P A S M E W I A
R P A L F E M M C T E C M
M H P T L H N K T V M K C
C I C O A M E O Y V A E O
K I I R T T C H A R R N R
Y A D H T L C B U C S S E
R Y Y Y A R E K C A H T Y
```

- ALCOTT
- BAGNOLD
- BECKETT
- CHARTERIS
- COREY
- DICKENS
- HARDY
- KINGSLEY
- KIPLING
- LEASOR
- MANTEL
- MARSH
- PLAIDY
- PRICE
- PROUST
- THACKERAY
- TOLKIEN
- WHEATLEY

76 Cartoon Characters

```
T  B  I  H  Q  F  X  T  O  T  D  R  J
R  F  B  Z  P  X  A  I  U  E  B  E  F
E  R  M  D  M  C  H  R  K  X  F  P  Q
B  E  A  R  P  C  W  I  D  E  N  M  U
L  D  B  O  C  U  P  P  I  R  O  U  T
I  F  T  O  A  S  O  P  E  A  S  H  H
D  L  N  P  U  P  Y  N  D  P  P  T  E
G  I  K  Y  E  T  N  V  P  H  M  O  G
P  N  G  Y  E  U  Y  A  J  A  I  T  R
Z  T  E  E  R  S  M  N  M  E  S  U  I
T  S  W  D  D  S  K  O  Y  L  A  L  N
T  T  A  V  L  N  S  W  W  A  S  P  C
H  O  T  G  A  O  X  C  C  G  I  O  H
R  N  C  N  L  W  B  U  B  B  L  E  S
C  E  T  J  Z  Y  H  Z  E  J  N  I  H
```

- BAMBI
- BUBBLES
- DILBERT
- DROOPY
- FRED FLINTSTONE
- LISA SIMPSON

- MOWGLI
- PINOCCHIO
- PLUTO
- POPEYE
- RAPHAEL
- ROAD RUNNER

- SNOWY
- SPIKE
- THE GRINCH
- THUMPER
- TOP CAT
- TWEETY PIE

77   Calendar

```
Y U L Y C A R E G S V P E
K S T N E D I M U A S N R
Y R A U R B E F C K U E S
E J N I C W P I E J B E F
K V E A N R V E N O T J Y
S E S L I T W S T A H O K
L H S A Y R S C D E R F N
Y W T S M N O D L N M W O
A U G N O T N G A G T T O
S L Q S O H S E E Y Q S M
E A A U C M B I W R S U L
R E P R N A M O R Y G G L
S Z A R Y A M Z L H E U U
L M E X I I O U N T C A F
N J A G M L J A M I U F R
```

- APRIL
- AUGUST
- CHRISTMAS
- DATES
- FEBRUARY
- FULL MOON

- GREGORIAN
- JULY
- JUNE
- MARCH
- MAY
- MONTHS

- NEW YEAR
- OCTOBER
- ROMAN
- SAINTS' DAYS
- SEASONS
- WEEKS

78 Things That Flow

H	A	M	I	N	V	G	W	A	V	E	S	C
L	A	E	S	H	N	R	E	Y	G	N	E	G
I	R	I	P	P	L	E	H	Y	E	T	D	N
O	S	P	A	R	O	G	F	J	S	T	I	I
E	M	U	E	L	O	R	T	E	P	E	T	S
L	O	U	D	F	W	A	T	E	R	M	R	S
B	K	O	R	O	E	V	S	X	V	A	A	E
A	E	R	C	C	O	Y	I	T	W	G	L	R
T	A	D	I	L	X	L	Y	L	E	M	I	D
E	R	U	H	V	O	W	B	E	C	A	D	D
G	J	I	H	Z	U	U	C	M	D	B	M	A
E	L	M	C	N	N	L	D	I	U	Q	I	L
V	D	A	A	K	S	P	E	S	K	F	R	A
U	V	T	B	O	L	U	T	T	W	E	F	S
I	G	R	A	Y	G	E	Q	U	E	R	A	C

- BLOOD
- CLOUDS
- GEYSER
- GRAVY
- JUICE
- LIQUID
- MAGMA
- PETROLEUM
- RIPPLE
- RIVULET
- SALAD DRESSING
- SMOKE
- STEAM
- TIDES
- TRICKLE
- VEGETABLE OIL
- WATER
- WAVES

79 Moon Craters

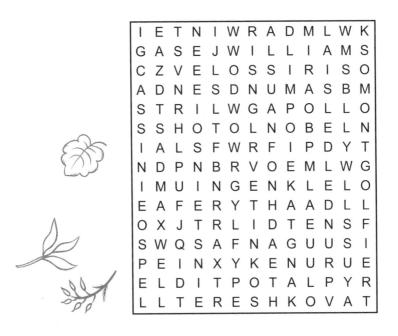

```
I E T N I W R A D M L W K
G A S E J W I L L I A M S
C Z V E L O S S I R I S O
A D N E S D N U M A S B M
S T R I L W G A P O L L O
S S H O T O L N O B E L N
I A L S F W R F I P D Y T
N D P N B R V O E M L W G
I M U I N G E N K L E L O
E A F E R Y T H A A D L L
O X J T R L I D T E N S F
S W Q S A F N A G U U S I
P E I N X Y K E N U R U E
E L D I T P O T A L P Y R
L L T E R E S H K O V A T
```

- AMUNDSEN
- APOLLO
- CASSINI
- DARWIN
- EINSTEIN
- FLEMING

- FREUD
- KOROLEV
- MAXWELL
- MONTGOLFIER
- NOBEL
- OSIRIS

- PENTLAND
- PLATO
- RUTHERFORD
- TERESHKOVA
- TYNDALL
- WILLIAMS

80 Harvest Time

```
G B E L A H T B I A M N R
A R F H C G M R I S E E L
S S A T W C O A A A D S N
G A R P G L U F T I U R F
O H M E E H S P C U L J V
L A Y V W S E A G R E E K
T E A M W O R K N J G H R
E H R J W Y L Y T N E L P
Y E D A O E M F I J D S D
S H U G S N U R I L I T E
C A D E R O E S E L B A S
R E P P O H E I A R U W E
O E A I T G Y G E E U A O
P R H A W H E A T S N Z C
S A G Y A F D H W A G O N
```

- BREAD
- CAULI-
  FLOWERS
- CIDER
- CROPS
- FARMYARD
- FRUITFUL
- GATHERING
- GRAPES
- HONEY
- HOPPER
- MOUSE
- PLENTY
- SILAGE
- TEAMWORK
- TRAILER
- WAGON
- WHEAT
- YIELD

To become different
from what we are,
we must have
some awareness
of what we are.

Eric Hoffer

81 Things That Go Round

```
Z A R U K E M M E S E T L
I L M S H O X D I P N R A
J D I Q Z U P D R M O T C
V H N V Y H L E Y J O S E
W B S U Y U L A A F M H G
Q K C O O L E E H W D L Y
R P Y S O R T Y I O R R R
O O C R L L O N X K O N O
T G L H E U D G F Y C P S
S O O B D M V C Y O E M C
A K N S I S P G M R R A O
C A E L E K C E R F R O P
F R L W R Z T I H E A E E
J T G U D P L A N E T V M
R E X I M T N E M E C Y B
```

- CASTOR
- CEMENT MIXER
- COMET
- CYCLONE
- DREIDEL
- FAN BELT
- GO-KART
- GYROSCOPE
- HULA HOOP
- MERRY-GO-ROUND
- MOON
- PLANET
- RECORD
- ROLLER
- WHEEL
- WHISK
- WINDMILL
- YO-YO

82 Artists

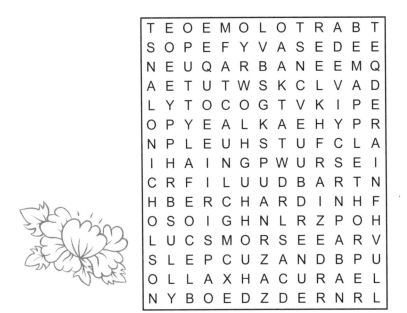

```
T E O E M O L O T R A B T
S O P E F Y V A S E D E E
N E U Q A R B A N E E M Q
A E T U T W S K C L V A D
L Y T O C O G T V K I P E
O P Y E A L K A E H Y P R
N P L E U H S T U F C L A
I H A I N G P W U R S E I
C R F I L U U D B A R T N
H B E R C H A R D I N H F
O S O I G H N L R Z P O H
L U C S M O R S E E A R V
S L E P C U Z A N D B P U
O L L A X H A C U R A E L
N Y B O E D Z D E R N R L
```

- BACON
- BARTOLOMEO
- BERRUGUETE
- BOSCH
- BRAQUE
- CHARDIN

- DAUMIER
- DELAUNEY
- DERAIN
- DUFY
- KLEE
- LOWRY

- MAPPLE-THORPE
- MORSE
- NICHOLSON
- NOLAN
- PENCZ
- SULLY

83 Lakes

```
L B A P E D K D Y E L R R
A M L F A C Y E I H E M A
B E O T P U D O I R A N B
A M M W U W M S L S H F I
Z N O V A R A A G E N O M
I U N R J A K E S E R O L
A V D A K A N A J M E M P
L E R S Z E E A N L K A I
V O N A G U L D Z A S H Y
T H J A J M B S A I M A A
T A R V Z I U K N Z U A E
R T D E K O S S O U S E C
K W A N I A O A V O T Z B
K L L E W O P K N K T A I
Y O G G E P J N O R U H G
```

- DOIRAN
- EDWARD
- GATUN
- GENEVA
- HURON
- IHEMA

- IZABAL
- KOSSOU
- KWANIA
- LOMOND
- LUGANO
- NASIJARVI

- OHRID
- ONEGA
- POWELL
- SAIMAA
- TAHOE
- TURKANA

84 Bridges

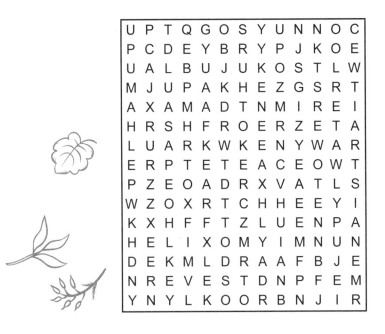

```
U P T Q G O S Y U N N O C
P C D E Y B R Y P J K O E
U A L B U J U K O S T L W
M J U P A K H E Z G S R T
A X A M A D T N M I R E I
H R S H F R O E R Z E T A
L U A R K W K E N Y W A R
E R P T E T E A C E O W T
P Z E O A D R X V A T L S
W Z O X R T C H H E E Y I
K X H F F T Z L U E N P A
H E L I X O M Y I M N U N
D E K M L D R A A F B J E
N R E V E S T D N P F E M
Y N Y L K O O R B N J I R
```

- BROOKLYN
- DEER ISLE
- HELIX
- HUMBER
- JAMSU
- KHAJU
- KOTHUR
- MENAI STRAIT
- PARK AVENUE
- PEACE
- PELHAM
- PORT MANN
- RED CLIFF
- REXFORD
- SEVERN
- TATARA
- TOWER
- WATERLOO

85 Orchestral Instruments

```
T W E N O H P O L Y X E R
Z U O C C A S T A N E T S
G J B O E S T I E N E N W
U L Y U D L A O A N D I A
I G O E L B E O D E R L V
T V K C M A L S N P P O I
T G S I K M R O T A I I C
A I R L I E B B C A C V O
T A M T A M N R E K C K N
M O M P O B H S G L O O A
W W A R A L M U P Y L D I
A K T Z S N I Y S I O S P
R M F B Q T I A C R E T P
E C O R A N G L A I S L R
S X N R O H H C N E R F E
```

- CASTANETS
- CELESTA
- COR ANGLAIS
- CORNET
- CYMBALS
- FRENCH HORN
- GLOCKENSPIEL
- GUITAR
- MARIMBA
- PIANO
- PICCOLO
- TAM-TAM
- TIMPANI
- TROMBONE
- TUBULAR BELLS
- VIOLIN
- WOOD BLOCK
- XYLOPHONE

86　Grasses

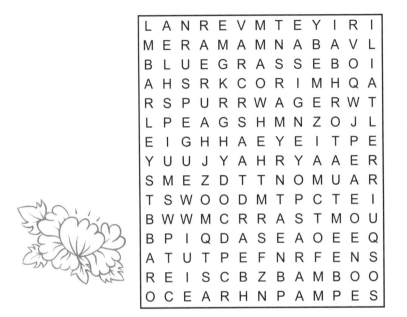

```
L A N R E V M T E Y I R I
M E R A M A M N A B A V L
B L U E G R A S S E B O I
A H S R K C O R I M H Q A
R S P U R R W A G E R W T
L P E A G S H M N Z O J L
E I G H H A E Y E I T P E
Y U U J Y A H R Y A A E R
S M E Z D T T N O M U A R
T S W O O D M T P C T E I
B W W M C R R A S T M O U
B P I Q D A S E A O E E Q
A T U T P E F N R F E N S
R E I S C B Z B A M B O O
O C E A R H N P A M P E S
```

- BAMBOO
- BARLEY
- BEARD
- BLUEGRASS
- BROME
- ESPARTO

- FESCUE
- MAIZE
- MEADOW
- PAMPAS
- RATTAN
- SORGHUM

- SQUIRRELTAIL
- SUGAR CANE
- TIMOTHY
- TWITCH
- VERNAL
- WHEAT

87 Wild Flowers

```
A R I N E F N C R A N E E
V A L W O A E P P X D M R
F H Y Z I E I D M A A Q U
R P O T Q L T S I V N L Q
A T N N X R L S D E M S F
J E B O E E Y O U T A Y Y
G L C F F Y T E W C H O F
M O O T A K S I M H M P R
B I S T O R T U N K E O O
L V E R V A I N C O C R G
W E Y W R E E R T K C F B
U K O C U D W E E D L A I
W A G T V N H T N H H E T
D F F U F E E S L F Y M Q
W O A T A S B A C R U C S
```

- ACONITE
- ASTER
- BISTORT
- CUDWEED
- DAISY
- FLAX
- FROGBIT
- GENTIAN
- HONEYSUCKLE
- OXLIP
- PANSY
- ROCKET
- TREFOIL
- VERVAIN
- VETCH
- VIOLET
- WILLOWHERB
- WOAD

88 Famous New Zealanders

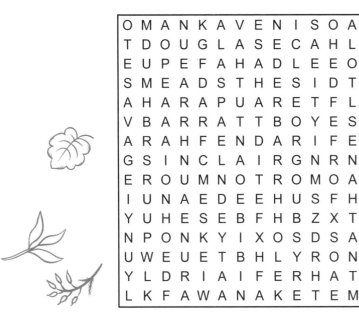

```
O M A N K A V E N I S O A
T D O U G L A S E C A H L
E U P E F A H A D L E E O
S M E A D S T H E S I D T
A H A R A P U A R E T F L
V B A R R A T T B O Y E S
A R A H F E N D A R I F E
G S I N C L A I R G N R N
E R O U M N O T R O M O A
I U N A E D E E H U S F H
Y U H E S E B F H B Z X T
N P O N K Y I X O S D S A
U W E U E T B H L Y R O N
Y L D R I A I F E R H A T
L K F A W A N A K E T E M
```

- AITKEN
- BARRATT-BOYES
- DOUGLAS
- FRAME
- FREYBERG
- HADLEE
- HOBSON
- MARSH
- MEADS
- MORTON
- NATHAN
- NGATA
- SAVAGE
- SINCLAIR
- SNELL
- TE KANAWA
- TE RAUPARAHA
- UPHAM

89 Spring Bouquet

```
Y L I L B E R U F U M S I
M A R Y C A N E M O N E Y
U L T E L I D O F F A D A
S U C O R C I R I S R E I
P A N I O A C I A F C S S
R E R A C F S A B B I O E
A F R H P H S E H R S R E
V L Z I D X U T A A S M R
Y P L J W T N C L A U I F
I U T I E I S J S O S R R
T C E L C U N A E E C P Y
K A O A M S E K R E R F G
I I Y U A R A L L I U M T
V H N E C A P S F E R O A
E V O L G X O F Y S N A P
```

- ALLIUM
- ANEMONE
- COLTSFOOT
- CROCUS
- DAFFODIL
- FOXGLOVE

- FREESIA
- HYACINTH
- IRIS
- LILY
- MUSCARI
- NARCISSUS

- PANSY
- PERIWINKLE
- PRIMROSE
- SCILLA
- TULIP
- VIOLET

90 Not on a Diet

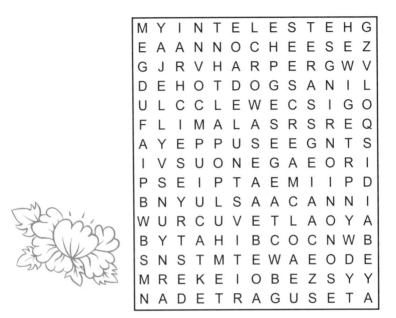

```
M Y I N T E L E S T E H G
E A A N N O C H E E S E Z
G J R V H A R P E R G W V
D E H O T D O G S A N I L
U L C C L E W E C S I G O
F L I M A L A S R S R E Q
A Y E P P U S E E G N T S
I V S U O N E G A E O R I
P S E I P T A E M I I P D
B N Y U L S A A C A N N I
W U R C U V E T L A O Y A
B Y T A H I B C O C N W B
S N S T M T E W A E O D E
M R E K E I O B E Z S Y Y
N A D E T R A G U S E T A
```

- ALCOHOL
- BACON
- BUTTER
- CANDY
- CHEESE
- CREAM
- ECLAIRS
- FUDGE
- HOT DOGS
- JELLY
- MEAT PIES
- ONION RINGS
- POTATOES
- ROLLS
- SALAMI
- SAUSAGES
- SUGAR
- SYRUP

91   Varieties of Tomato

```
I A M F O R E N Z Y N J A
A D A S O R A W G E U R C
B A O L J A Y L C D U P Y
A I S O O R K T E K A M A
P M G Y U R A S A G G T H
A I A B T R R S R Y E A J
M J C R O T P E P C T N R
Y E A C O Y E W H A G E D
R N S O O N O M L C O J H
I A N C Z L C R A T U N E
A U Y E L M O T A L I A D
D E B E J S J M I N F P N
E R Y L W D I E C Q J E A
A J R A F N T A E E Y R E
A W A M A K S E L R I O S
```

- APERO

- BIG BOY

- CHERROLA

- FLAME

- GREEN ZEBRA

- INCAS

- JENNY

- JULIET

- LATAH

- LEGEND

- MYRIADE

- NECTAR

- ORAMA

- PICCOLO

- ROSADA

- SAKURA

- TAMINA

- YELLOW
  PYGMY

92 Jewels and Trinkets

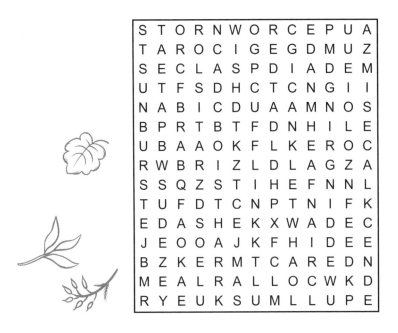

```
S T O R N W O R C E P U A
T A R O C I G E G D M U Z
S E C L A S P D I A D E M
U T F S D H C T C N G I I
N A B I C D U A A M N O S
B P R T B T F D N H I L E
U B A A O K F L K E R O C
R W B R I Z L D L A G Z A
S S Q Z S T I H E F N N L
T U F D T C N P T N I F K
E D A S H E K X W A D E C
J E O O A J K F H I D E E
B Z K E R M T C A R E D N
M E A L R A L L O C W K D
R Y E U K S U M L L U P E
```

- ANKLET
- BEADS
- CHAIN
- CHOKER
- CLASP
- COLLAR

- CROWN
- CUFFLINK
- DIADEM
- HATPIN
- LOCKET
- NECKLACE

- PEARLS
- SUNBURST
- TIARA
- TORQUE
- WATCH
- WEDDING RING

93 Salad

```
T U S E S H E R A P P A S
E S E E H C A G O E I V I
U S R C D J N C A R R O T
D M C A H I R S A B E O U
E X U E S I R M O T B T X
F L V S L E V J T Z K A A
R U E I M E A E N T N C
O R Y N C O R C S E U O N
D N S R N G O Y E Z S L O
L I R N I E C R I A C B T
A C L A O V F M H A V S U
W O N E D I D P E S B P O
N I S A R I N I A R U Z R
V S T I M H S O E G B M C
Z E W A S D E H E R A P G
```

- CABBAGE
- CAESAR
- CARROT
- CELERY
- CHEESE
- CHIVES

- CROUTON
- DRESSING
- FENNEL
- HERBS
- MIZUNA
- MUSHROOMS

- NICOISE
- ONIONS
- PEAS
- RADISH
- VINAIGRETTE
- WALDORF

A perception, sudden
as blinking, that
subject and object
are one, will lead to
a deeply mysterious
understanding;
and by this
understanding
you will awaken
to the truth.

Huangbo Xiyun

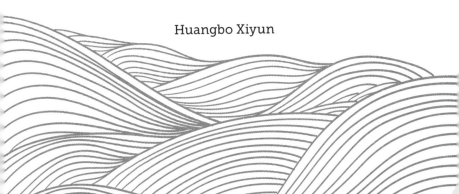

94 Abide With Me

```
A S E N I L A R A G E M K
D R U D P W L F A A L P V
P L N R A R L E V J L T L
U N I I V U E O W P E F C
T O T V U I D T W D O C R
U T N S E Y V R H L R E T
P P O E G O J E I E M M N
W E C D X H N L N A S W T
I C I I N H A B I T E U N
T C P S S T A N D F O R V
H A P E R S I S T K B O L
K O O R B E M A C B E D O
H A T T E N D I D A V E D
R E F F U S T F M L U T G
U S E V A S E T T L E O E
```

- ACCEPT
- ATTEND
- AWAIT
- BROOK
- CONTINUE
- DWELL

- INHABIT
- LIVE ON
- LODGE
- PERSIST
- PUT UP WITH
- REMAIN

- RESIDE
- SETTLE
- STAND FOR
- STICK OUT
- SUFFER
- SURVIVE

95 Deserts

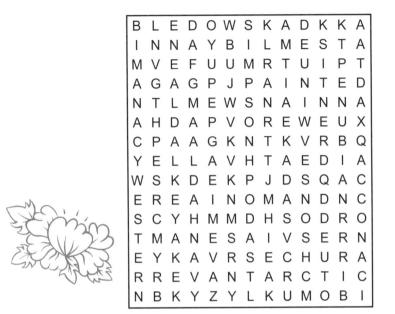

```
B L E D O W S K A D K K A
I N N A Y B I L M E S T A
M V E F U U M R T U I P T
A G A G P J P A I N T E D
N T L M E W S N A I N N A
A H D A P V O R E W E U X
C P A A G K N T K V R B Q
Y E L L A V H T A E D I A
W S K D E K P J D S Q A C
E R E A I N O M A N D N C
S C Y H M M D H S O D R O
T M A N E S A I V S E R N
E Y K A V R S E C H U R A
R R E V A N T A R C T I C
N B K Y Z Y L K U M O B I
```

- ACCONA
- AL-DAHNA
- ANTARCTIC
- BLEDOWSKA
- DEATH VALLEY
- HALENDI

- KYZYLKUM
- LIBYAN
- MOJAVE
- NAMIB
- NEGEV
- NUBIAN

- ORDOS
- PAINTED
- SAHARA
- SECHURA
- SIMPSON
- WESTERN

Famous Buildings and Monuments

```
F E M A D E R T O N R C S
S L A P E D R E R A H P X
W P L B B E L A G A U H A
S H A R U V K R R I T N E
U I C C G S A M E S G A R
A L S D E F I D W K F R E
H L A Q O N R M O S E B C
U H L R A O E R B C M M H
A O T R C W W E H E S A T
B U F H E A O E D B L H H
Q S C L T R T T M L K L E
U E U K A K N I K O E A I
A O R K U K C S A R H P O
Y K R E M L I N E T O G N
S L A M X U R T I Y U W N
```

- ABU SIMBEL
- AGRA FORT
- ALHAMBRA
- ANGKOR WAT
- BAUHAUS
- CHARMINAR
- CN TOWER
- ERECHTHEION
- HILL HOUSE
- HOMEWOOD
- KINKAKU
- KREMLIN
- LA PEDRERA
- LA SCALA
- NOTRE DAME
- SPACE NEEDLE
- TIKAL
- UXMAL

```
S G C E S O R L E M R P S
G R E L E D I S Y A T E A
A V K E A L M P A M B R G
S L Y W L N D B L L W T R
P O C I P X S P K V M H U
N W U S K H A G G I S O I
S A I N T A N D R E W L N
Y H P O D F I R N K C A A
S A L A L O J V N C V M R
T M S K G R F P X I O L D
I H P M K F L S E W R A B
F T U I I A P M L R S S A
X E L R I R O P Y E O H Y
V T B D S R G T V L A C X
S N D B E O S O M H V T D
```

- AVIEMORE
- CLANS
- FORFAR
- GRIMSAY
- GRUINARD BAY
- HAGGIS

- KILTS
- LAMLASH
- LERWICK
- LEWIS
- MELROSE
- PERTH

- PLAID
- SAINT ANDREW
- SALMON
- SOUND OF SLEAT
- TAYSIDE
- THURSO

98 Sports Equipment

E	T	R	I	A	R	R	E	I	R	T	E	H
A	N	E	C	A	W	O	T	A	K	E	L	H
B	B	E	K	J	P	A	A	S	T	R	A	V
U	R	A	A	S	I	R	K	H	E	R	G	H
C	O	C	T	K	A	S	S	T	O	L	S	A
S	K	J	B	T	G	B	F	M	O	S	T	O
S	I	U	E	Y	L	V	L	V	K	T	S	E
H	D	E	A	L	N	E	E	I	C	E	O	C
R	E	A	U	I	R	S	D	H	U	N	P	J
U	E	G	P	E	G	E	G	O	P	F	L	P
T	E	N	W	E	I	K	V	N	R	V	A	U
Z	E	F	V	L	E	H	S	I	I	E	O	T
T	R	U	C	J	F	N	S	G	U	R	G	T
F	A	S	O	R	E	N	K	A	M	Q	P	E
S	A	S	F	F	A	N	K	L	M	I	E	R

- BASKET
- BATTLEDORE
- ETRIER
- GLOVES
- GOALPOSTS
- JACK

- KNEE-PADS
- LUGE
- MASHIE
- NETS
- OARS
- PUCK

- PUTTER
- QUIVER
- RINGS
- SCUBA
- SKATE
- TENPIN

99   Made of Glass

```
T S Z E N E C N I P A P R
O H I C T E L T T O B R E
V R G W A T C H F A C E M
E E R I N C E N E Z N M I
N T L D E D Y P N E K I S
W E D I F W N E I R S T R
A M S E G E R R J P A G A
R O T U M B L E R H L G L
E M O E O U I E P N F E U
L R I I S H I B T A M O C
R E L R H T N R E A P N O
B H N A R E T E A A Z I N
A T E S U O L U E U K B I
U A B D E S R Y B R Q E B
Y A R T H S A H D E G A R
```

- AQUARIUM

- ASHTRAY

- BEAKER

- BINOCULARS

- BOTTLE

- EGG TIMER

- FLASK

- GREENHOUSE

- LENSES

- MIRROR

- OVENWARE

- PAPERWEIGHT

- PINCE-NEZ

- PIPETTE

- TEST TUBE

- THER-
  MOMETER

- TUMBLER

- WATCH FACE

100 Hues

```
K R I Z E S A N E N A A G
W O L L E Y N F V E L V E
H F L A E N O T S E S O F
O Y T Z V P N F U R I C E
Z E O U E N I R E G N A T
A S K R R W U F Y R D D A
I M B E O Q O M D J I O S
S L E M U N U E I J G T T
H E L I O T R O P E O E I
C X B M N D L E I Y S R E
U D E R O C A Q I S N A C
F L I O O C E I U E E L E
U S L P H N O R S N V C P
E B O N Y G Z H E P U A A
P A R E A T S E N P H E D
```

- AVOCADO
- AZURE
- BLOOD RED
- BRONZE
- CLARET
- EBONY
- FUCHSIA
- GREEN
- HELIOTROPE
- INDIGO
- LEMON
- PEACH
- PUCE
- RUSSET
- STONE
- TANGERINE
- TURQUOISE
- YELLOW

101 Rainy Day

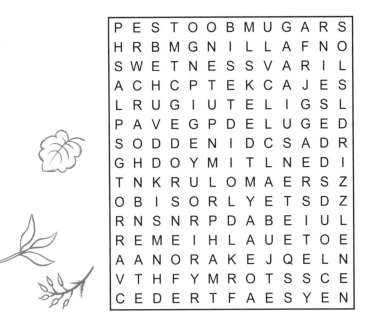

```
P E S T O O B M U G A R S
H R B M G N I L L A F N O
S W E T N E S S V A R I L
A C H C P T E K C A J E S
L R U G I U T E L I G S L
P A V E G P D E L U G E D
S O D D E N I D C S A D R
G H D O Y M I T L N E D I
T N K R U L O M A E R S Z
O B I S O R L Y E T S D Z
R N S N R P D A B E I U L
R E M E I H L A U E T O E
A A N O R A K E J Q E L N
V T H F Y M R O T S S C E
C E D E R T F A E S Y E N
```

- ANORAK
- CLOUDS
- DELUGE
- DRIZZLE
- DROPLETS
- FALLING
- GUMBOOTS
- JACKET
- PRE-CIPITATION
- PUDDLES
- RAINING
- SODDEN
- SPLASH
- SQUALLY
- STORMY
- TEEMING
- TORRENT
- WETNESS

102 Art Media

```
E O V I N A L F S E H A N
T S A O S R E R N O C H O
A S D M E I R G S K T B Y
R E O K L F W T L R E M A
E G R E S O N A S F K O R
P A R N O I H T K C S S C
M E A D A C E N K I T A B
E R C P B N I N R A C I R
T U L C C D G B I R P C E
T I E I N O A I Y L Y V E
O Y L A R L Z L I T T V R
S Y N Y F Y I L T B U U S
T E N E H C A U O G E P O
P S A Y W K P B L C V A H
P E O F S R E F S N A R T
```

- ACRYLIC
- BATIK
- CHALK
- CRAYON
- GESSO
- GOUACHE
- MARKER
- MOSAIC
- OIL PAINTS
- OUTLINE
- PEN AND INK
- PUTTY
- RELIEF
- SKETCH
- STENCIL
- TEMPERA
- TRANSFERS
- WOODCUT

103 Safari Park

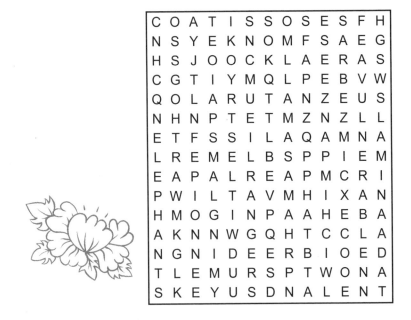

```
C O A T I S S O S E S F H
N S Y E K N O M F S A E G
H S J O O C K L A E R A S
C G T I Y M Q L P E B V W
Q O L A R U T A N Z E U S
N H N P T E T M Z N Z L L
E T F S S I L A Q A M N A
L R E M E L B S P P I E M
E A P A L R E A P M C R I
P W I L T A V M H I X A N
H M O G I N P A A H E B A
A K N N W G Q H T C C L A
N G N I D E E R B I O E D
T L E M U R S P T W O N A
S K E Y U S D N A L E N T
```

- ANIMALS
- BREEDING
- CAMELS
- CHIMPANZEES
- COATIS
- CON-SERVATION
- ELANDS
- ELEPHANTS
- HABITAT
- LEMURS
- LIONS
- LLAMAS
- MONKEYS
- NATURAL
- RANGERS
- VULNERABLE
- WARTHOGS
- ZEBRAS

104 Diamonds

```
S A V M V E C N W O R C A
E H B W A A M D A R U B H
L E I C R D E L E S N C S
D E I A L H R F L R I U S
R I T X S T L E S A F L E
I S F I H E G M T F O L N
G Y L G C Q U T I S R I D
B O I T S J E M P N M N R
P E I S B C A A V O I A A
W O E O A R R C E S T N H
N H T F Q K L R J U Y G G
Z A N U L U E S E E U V E
J M I E C O H W M O W E T
P S A R U N B I R M E E J
E B E L B A U L A V R B L
```

- AMSTERDAM
- CARATS
- CROWN
- CULLINAN
- FACET
- GIRDLE
- HARDNESS
- JEWEL
- MARQUISE
- MINING
- POLISHED
- REFLECTION
- ROUGH
- SPARKLE
- UNCUT
- UNIFORMITY
- VALUABLE
- WEIGHT

105 Classical Music Titles

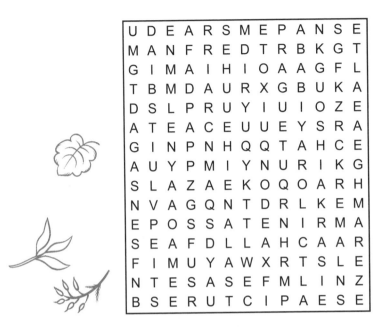

```
U D E A R S M E P A N S E
M A N F R E D T R B K G T
G I M A I H I O A A G F L
T B M D A U R X G B U K A
D S L P R U Y I U I O Z E
A T E A C E U U E Y S R A
G I N P N H Q Q T A H C E
A U Y P M I Y N U R I K G
S L A Z A E K O Q O A R H
N V A G Q N T D R L K E M
E P O S S A T E N I R M A
S E A F D L L A H C A A R
F I M U Y A W X R T S L E
N T E S A S E F M L I N Z
B S E R U T C I P A E S E
```

- *ANTAR*
- *BABI YAR*
- *BLANIK*
- *DON QUIXOTE*
- *EN SAGA*
- *EROICA*

- *LA MER*
- *LINZ*
- *MANFRED*
- *MARS*
- *PRAGUE*
- *SARKA*

- *SEA PICTURES*
- *SWAN LAKE*
- *TABOR*
- *TASSO*
- *THE TEMPEST*
- *URANUS*

106 Orchestral Music

```
F E S M A N S R G U T Y W
A A N E R U T R E V O L N
D W O R T Y U B M D A D E
G N I N U T E D O V A K A
I E T M E S N D R S G E Y
E N C B C I N E J B S T L
S O E A W E T J C S R T R
T B S D C N R O A K E L E
A M O S I C N R R S Y E B
Y O E M H C B A C T A D M
W R P O E A F O N R L R A
C T R R T N R O A I P U H
M U T O S E E A R N R M C
S O N T E A R E E G E E A
R E S O P M O C E S N E T
```

- BATON
- BRASS
- CHAMBER
- CHORUS
- COMPOSER
- CONCERTO
- CRESCENDO
- INTERVAL
- KETTLEDRUM
- LEADER
- OVERTURE
- PLAYERS
- SCORE
- SECTIONS
- STRINGS
- TROMBONE
- TUNING
- WOODWIND

Meditation is not
about stopping
thoughts, but
recognizing that
we are more than
our thoughts and
our feelings.

Arianna Huffington

107 Rocks and Minerals

```
S A U N L T T B P M S W Y
E R M S G E C I M U P R T
J N I D J T R A O R E S Z
O C O G L U B E A M I R O
R A E C N E N E E H O G U
B S L L R E N N C X L R E
B N Q E I I O S E A Y A P
A E F T V T Z U U J E N N
G Y E I S A U L S D C O O
L N L T E R A R I P P S
A O L A A M S D O F S H K
T I C P H Z K V S L R Y L
S U S A R E P S A J O R P
X P F Y E F G T O H D E M
A I L F A N E L A G D A E
```

- APATITE
- EMERY
- GABBRO
- GALENA
- GRANOPHYRE
- IGNEOUS

- JASPER
- JET
- OLIVINE
- ONYX
- PUMICE
- RUTILE

- SCHIST
- SILTSTONE
- SLATE
- SPAR
- TUFF
- ZIRCON

108 Breakfast

```
D T S A O T A Y E N O H E
P E I K B S D O M B E W K
G A O A S A P R I C O T S
P G C A E D A D I C I X A
A O E R T C R U M D I W U
N H B D N M J B E A N S S
C O F F E E E D O J M H A
A M V T G H M A B I A R G
K W U N Y U C D L E R S E
E D A E F O L A A K M O S
S R D F S A G R O L A I V
O I I R F L W U W P L O T
V N M Y J L I V R Y A N A
S N E A F Z E T E T D S E
J N W O R B H S A H E H P
```

- APRICOTS
- BACON
- BEANS
- BREAD
- COFFEE
- HASH BROWN
- HONEY
- MARMALADE
- MUESLI
- MUFFINS
- OATMEAL
- ORANGE JUICE
- PANCAKES
- POACHED EGG
- SAUSAGES
- TOAST
- WAFFLES
- YOGURT

109 Plain and Simple

```
E L P M I S A O S E D L I
U E S E M E R E V L E U S
O A R Y T O T A Y E N F C
Q U A S M C D H C P R H U
E Y T Q U A E E E S E T T
F R T S L O G R S E T U H
C A E B P N I D I T T R G
A N W C E O E V O D A T I
N I A L N T K R B I P E R
D D I I U I R E T O N V N
I R T M J W S A N O U I W
D O N A T R A P S E M D O
U N E M B E L L I S H E D
E N R T V I S I B L E N L
G N I M U S S A N U A T E
```

- CANDID
- DIRECT
- DOWNRIGHT
- EVIDENT
- MODEST
- MUTED

- OBVIOUS
- ORDINARY
- OUTSPOKEN
- OVERT
- SIMPLE
- SINCERE

- SPARTAN
- TRUTHFUL
- UNASSUMING
- UNEM-
  BELLISHED
- UNPATTERNED
- VISIBLE

110 Pairs of Things

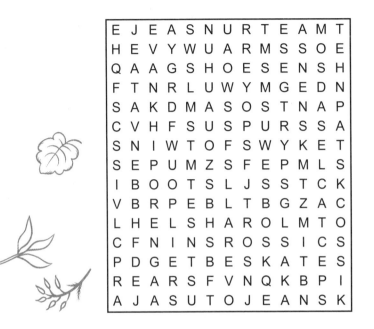

```
E J E A S N U R T E A M T
H E V Y W U A R M S S O E
Q A A G S H O E S E N S H
F T N R L U W Y M G E D N
S A K D M A S O S T N A P
C V H F S U S P U R S S A
S N I W T O F S W Y K E T
S E P U M Z S F E P M L S
I B O O T S L J S S T C K
V B R P E B L T B G Z A C
L H E L S H A R O L M T O
C F N I N S R O S S I C S
P D G E T B E S K A T E S
R E A R S F V N Q K B P I
A J A S U T O J E A N S K
```

- BOOTS
- CHROMO-SOMES
- EARMUFFS
- GLASSES
- HANDS
- JEANS
- OVERALLS
- PANTS
- PLIERS
- SCISSORS
- SHOES
- SKATES
- SOCKS
- SPECTACLES
- SPURS
- STAYS
- TONGS
- TWINS

111 Chess

```
K A G I B S O R W A M V E
Y E T E C A J H G C O X T
P N S T O S I L R R V F N
K W O K L T E P A G E U E
P A P I E Y O P N A S W M
W P T N M H S K D M T N A
R D U G S A C M M B G I N
Y U O I K A L E A I M E R
K L B M T H E V S T J D U
N R O T X D F E T P T A O
I G A V S N R S E L M K T
G Y R M E O S I R H Z C R
H S D I N A V E A P N O U
T A T S Y I O A T M O L J
K A M E R W K W D K W B O
```

- ATTACK
- BISHOP
- BLOCKADE
- BOARD
- GAMBIT
- GRAND-MASTER
- KASPAROV
- KING
- KNIGHT
- KRAMNIK
- MOVES
- OUTPOST
- PAWN
- RESIGN
- ROOK
- RUBTSOVA
- TOURNAMENT
- WHITE

112 Shades of Blue

```
T E N I L U Z A L J C C R
U O U E M F L E D E R O U
F E E L U A R K L A R B C
T T M B T O J E R U Z A I
S E L M B R S O N H M L R
S M E R S T A O R C Y T T
O E A S E M O M N E H I C
I D N O B E T F A X L M E
R D U M A Z H P N R Y L L
D L A P H L G A R V I S E
E E G Y P T I A N U I N U
N K C E U S R E J O U T E
I G L I R S B R O Y A L V
M N A E L U R E C L V E G
U U P A L A L G A R E T I
```

- ALICE
- AZURE
- BONDI
- BRIGHT
- CELESTE
- CERULEAN

- COBALT
- DENIM
- EGYPTIAN
- ELECTRIC
- FRENCH
- LAZULINE

- MAJORELLE
- PERSIAN
- ROYAL
- STEEL
- TUFTS
- ULTRAMARINE

113 Under the Ground

```
S E L F F U R T I U N L F
G B A R I N E V T V B E W
G O T U J T W S C E M N Y
Z L L N K U N O V S O N S
S H P D I B E A R F C U A
L A G E H E C E I M A T V
A B M R Y R P O N U T V M
R H Q P M H A D E S A Y S
E F Z A K L T U A A C L E
N C O S I L R E Q E M R D
I O O S U C J U L U R R A
M B S A P W I I D O A Z M
H O V M L F U D N I M C P
F Y I M E M F F N F S Y W
E V A R N U E P M A G M A
```

- AQUIFER
- CATACOMB
- CAVE
- COAL
- DRAIN
- FOSSIL

- GOLD
- HADES
- MAGMA
- MINERALS
- MOLE
- MYCELIUM

- TRUFFLES
- TUBER
- TUNNEL
- UNDERPASS
- VAULT
- WORM

114 Wake Up

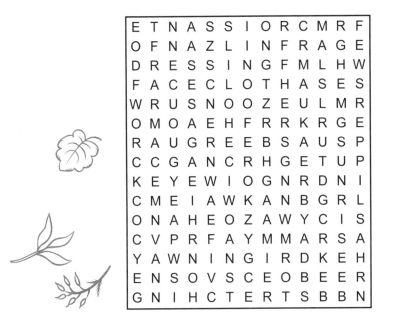

```
E T N A S S I O R C M R F
O F N A Z L I N F R A G E
D R E S S I N G F M L H W
F A C E C L O T H A S E S
W R U S N O O Z E U L M R
O M O A E H F R R K R G E
R A U G R E E B S A U S P
C C G A N C R H G E T U P
K E Y E W I O G N R D N I
C M E I A W K A N B G R L
O N A H E O Z A W Y C I S
C V P R F A Y M M A R S A
Y A W N I N G I R D K E H
E N S O V S C E O B E E R
G N I H C T E R T S B B N
```

- ARISE
- AWAKEN
- BED-MAKING
- CEREAL
- COCK-CROW
- CROISSANT

- DAYBREAK
- DRESSING
- FACE CLOTH
- GET UP
- HAIRBRUSH
- MUESLI

- SHOWER
- SLIPPERS
- SNOOZE
- STRETCHING
- SUNRISE
- YAWNING

115 TAIL Endings

```
C L E P C P L I A T E R L
U I I A I L O G D C A I I
R A O A S N P N O L A A A
T T D E R I T T Y T K M T
A D S E G A T A X T E B U
I B E T I O R O I W A H L
L I A T N A F A C L N I H
J I H T A T W O T V A I L
L Z A O L I C A Q T G C I
L I U T R K L Z G H A E A
L L I A T N E N T T S I T
T L I A T R I A H A A X L
A G I A S R I A R T A I L
I L Y B P L R H D T A I L
L I A S M A R E S T A I L
```

- COCKTAIL
- COTTONTAIL
- CURTAIL
- DETAIL
- ENTAIL
- FANTAIL

- HAIRTAIL
- HIGHTAIL
- MARE'S TAIL
- OXTAIL
- PIGTAIL
- PINTAIL

- PONYTAIL
- RAT-TAIL
- RETAIL
- SHIRT TAIL
- SPRINGTAIL
- WAGTAIL

116 Birds of Prey

```
S A L U H O R O D N O C E
R L B E G O Y E A T F I A
E L G A E E B K E O S I Y
G P A Y T R N B R H A C H
E U N N C I A E Y B R H N
A Y G O L Y I L U E A I L
J G Q R C R S Z R R C C W
P L E G R L Z W K U A K O
O M E A R A A I U T R E N
N S H R R I H F O L A N R
D B P D T S F A S U C H A
O W K R B S V F R V Z A B
E E H M E U E I O S Z W T
L G S A O Y F K W N E K U
R E N N U R D A O R Y B A
```

- BARN OWL
- BESRA
- BUZZARD
- CARACARA
- CHICKEN HAWK
- CONDOR
- EAGLE
- FALCON
- GRIFFON
- HARRIER
- HOBBY
- JAEGER
- KESTREL
- MERLIN
- OSPREY
- ROADRUNNER
- SHIKRA
- VULTURE

117 Things We Love

S	T	R	I	N	E	S	C	S	H	Q	T	S
S	C	S	C	R	E	O	E	N	Y	O	L	B
H	U	G	N	A	I	I	E	L	F	O	G	C
C	A	N	D	Y	V	D	L	F	R	I	C	H
A	E	I	S	O	V	E	E	A	E	H	H	R
I	K	D	M	H	J	E	C	Y	O	O	J	I
R	C	D	C	H	I	S	E	C	A	K	E	S
C	L	E	A	S	P	N	O	R	E	U	E	T
O	I	W	C	O	E	L	E	X	P	S	A	M
C	F	S	E	R	A	S	A	D	N	E	G	A
A	Y	T	U	T	E	X	O	E	C	L	V	S
R	R	R	E	M	P	A	C	R	A	Z	O	M
Y	F	R	U	I	T	N	M	F	D	Z	F	E
T	E	L	E	V	I	S	I	O	N	U	R	D
R	A	M	I	N	A	L	I	S	R	P	A	E

- CAKES
- CANDY
- CAROLS
- CHOCOLATE
- CHRISTMAS
- FRUIT

- ICE CREAM
- INCENSE
- JELLY
- MUSIC
- OLD MOVIES
- POETRY

- PUZZLES
- ROSES
- SUNSHINE
- TELEVISION
- TOFFEE
- WEDDINGS

118 Paris Metro Stations

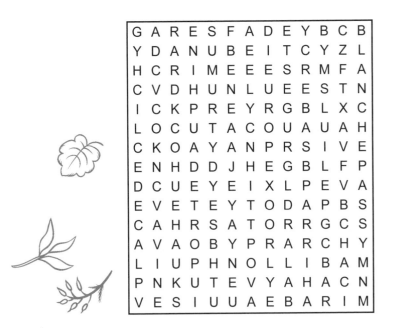

```
G A R E S F A D E Y B C B
Y D A N U B E I T C Y Z L
H C R I M E E E S R M F A
C V D H U N L U E E S T N
I C K P R E Y R G B L X C
L O C U T A C O U A U A H
C K O A Y A N P R S I V E
E N H D D J H E G B L F P
D C U E Y E I X L P E V A
E V E T E Y T O D A P B S
C A H R S A T O R R G C S
A V A O B Y P R A R C H Y
L I U P H N O L L I B A M
P N K U T E V Y A H A C N
V E S I U U A E B A R I M
```

- ALESIA
- BALARD
- BERCY
- BLANCHE
- CADET
- CHATELET
- CRIMEE
- DANUBE
- EUROPE
- MABILLON
- MIRABEAU
- PASSY
- PLACE DE CLICHY
- PORTE DAUPHINE
- RANELAGH
- SEGUR
- TOLBIAC
- VAVIN

119 Languages

```
H S I N N A D A N N A K C
O A H M R S R E T I P R I
T W V A C W W L E S S V V
P U B N F H D E N C I A S
A I A D R D I O D E A N E
C N G A E L I C T I A U D
I S T R N C U N H A S Z A
R T I I C R A I K E C H Y
I L A N H M W I H E W O F
M T B G E B R K O R E A N
H E A S A F E L O E R C E
S L E L A L I L I H A W S
A U S A I N O O L L A W S
K G H S I A L G A R P L E
V U K R O T N A R E P S E
```

- AFRIKAANS
- ARABIC
- CHICHEWA
- CREOLE
- ESPERANTO
- FRENCH

- GAELIC
- ITALIAN
- KANNADA
- KASHMIRI
- KOREAN
- MANDARIN

- SWAHILI
- SWEDISH
- TAGALOG
- TELUGU
- VIETNAMESE
- WALLOON

Without mind,
without meditation,
without analysis,
without practice,
without the will,
let it all be so.

Tilopa

```
E P R I N T E D D E L A L
S L E U R C U R E R H Y U
R E E R M C H E A R T H P
O L A I V N D S K M D E P
H G C M T Z T S F C A R E
S E P J S M K C B O O C L
R C W Z H N T A O C N L C
E M C A S T L E L I H O C
I A V U F L G A R A A Q F
D G I Q U E M P N C R U C
L I J U U A V D H S D E S
O C C B T E S E K E S Y Z
S A H I T O E Q I C H I V
I L O Y M O D N N I I V U
G N G E M B E B G S P L E
```

- BALL
- CASTLE
- CLOCK
- COACH
- CRUEL
- DRESS
- HANDSOME
- HARDSHIP
- HEARTH
- HORSE
- KING
- MAGICAL
- MICE
- PRINCE
- PROCLAMA-TION
- QUEEN
- RAGS
- SOLDIERS

121 Fun at the Fair

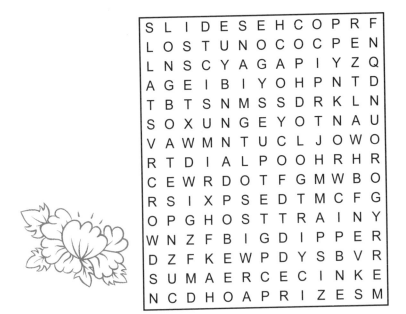

```
S L I D E S E H C O P R F
L O S T U N O C O C P E N
L N S C Y A G A P I Y Z Q
A G E I B I Y O H P N T D
T B T S N M S S D R K L N
S O X U N G E Y O T N A U
V A W M N T U C L J O W O
R T D I A L P O O H R H R
C E W R D O T F G M W B O
R S I X P S E D T M C F G
O P G H O S T T R A I N Y
W N Z F B I G D I P P E R
D Z F K E W P D Y S B V R
S U M A E R C E C I N K E
N C D H O A P R I Z E S M
```

- BIG DIPPER

- COCONUTS

- CROWDS

- GHOST TRAIN

- HOOPLA

- HOT DOG

- ICE CREAM

- LONGBOAT

- LOTS OF FUN

- MERRY-GO-ROUND

- MUSIC

- PIRATE SHIP

- POPCORN

- PRIZES

- SLIDES

- STALLS

- SWINGS

- WALTZER

122 Stimulating Words

```
A N E V I L N E E S I E E
F I Z T L E I S W K N B L
A I N E A R U A J C C K D
S U P F E G E V O B I V N
T M A E L G I U O A T C I
I E G A B A R T Q J E H K
V D E S I A M C S I S E L
P A B J G A G E A N P E A
E U F E F Y R G C J I R G
S S T Z E R R A Z F O N E
U R N P X S O P L I G L S
O E F O M E N T L L E H E
R P H U A E F R A L Y L K
A W A K E N T S N I Y C A
S A P E K O V O R P R E S
```

- AROUSE

- AWAKEN

- CAJOLE

- CHEER

- ENCOURAGE

- ENLIVEN

- FILLIP

- FOMENT

- IMPEL

- INCITE

- INFLAME

- INSTIGATE

- KINDLE

- PERSUADE

- PIQUE

- PROVOKE

- RALLY

- TEMPT

123 Goddesses

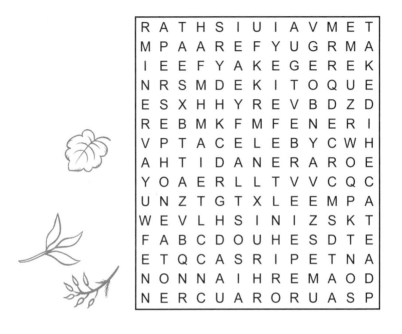

```
R A T H S I U I A V M E T
M P A A R E F Y U G R M A
I E E F Y A K E G E R E K
N R S M D E K I T O Q U E
E S X H H Y R E V B D Z D
R E B M K F M F E N E R I
V P T A C E L E B Y C W H
A H T I D A N E R A R O E
Y O A E R L L T V V C Q C
U N Z T G T X L E E M P A
W E V L H S I N I Z S K T
F A B C D O U H E S D T E
E T Q C A S R I P E T N A
N O N N A I H R E M A O D
N E R C U A R O R U A S P
```

- AMPHITRITE
- AURORA
- CALLISTO
- CYBELE
- DEMETER
- DURGA
- FREYA
- FRIGG
- HATHOR
- HECATE
- IRENE
- ISHTAR
- MESHKENT
- MINERVA
- PERSEPHONE
- RHIANNON
- VENUS
- VESTA

124 Astrology

```
U S P P S E R A O T E P A
R A T F R E M A G R E G W
A S E T A E A I R S I G N
R E A R T H D R I M O O N
B E P C S D U I V L D L B
I R A O T I I R C V E A D
L P E D C A U E L T K J T
R R F S I S Q H S E I B W
J E L E A N O C I S C O I
T C X H U Y G R C U I T N
A N B S E I L A O O L L S
U A R I E S I Y H H E T Y
R C C F E D H G H E L Y E
U S E B O S T G H W E G R
S A K Z O D A W N E S T A
```

- AIR SIGN
- ARCHER
- ARIES
- CANCER
- EARTH
- FISHES

- HOROSCOPE
- HOUSE
- LIBRA
- MOON
- PREDICTION
- READING

- STARS
- TAURUS
- TWINS
- VIRGO
- WHEEL
- ZODIAC

125 Brisk

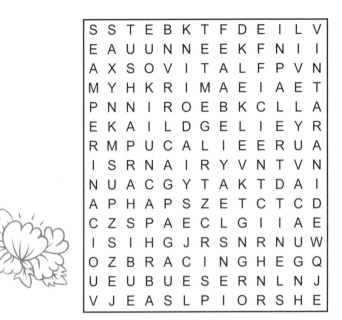

```
S S T E B K T F D E I L V
E A U U N N E E K F N I I
A X S O V I T A L F P V N
M Y H K R I M A E I A E T
P N N I R O E B K C L L A
E K A I L D G E L I E Y R
R M P U C A L I E E R U A
I S R N A I R Y V N T V N
N U A C G Y T A K T D A I
A P H A P S Z E T C T C D
C Z S P A E C L G I I A E
I S I H G J R S N R N U W
O Z B R A C I N G H E G Q
U E U B U E S E R N L N J
V J E A S L P I O R S H E
```

- AGILE
- ALERT
- BRACING
- BUSY
- CRISP
- EFFICIENT
- ENERGETIC
- EXHILARATING
- HASTY
- KEEN
- LIVELY
- NIMBLE
- QUICK
- SHARP
- SPIRITED
- VIGOROUS
- VITAL
- ZIPPY

126 Coffee

```
N H A L A M E T A U G S S
E O K A I V G R A T E T U
E U W U R M A R E S J M K
R S D H R B O T S A T C A
G E K L I M E C B T A E Y
E P C C E T D A H L M C N
B X A I Z N E M B A A H E
Y R T M N S J O Z F S T K
E H A R M A N R E K V O W
S J P Z A M G A Z I L O I
H S I R I C U R E A E M J
R C I H V L T T O B J S U
A E G T A X N I L R Y E P
L S W I Q A F W O I J A S
Y F T X M S T N E N H E R
```

- ARABICA
- AROMA
- BEANS
- BLACK
- BRAZIL
- CAFE AU LAIT
- EXTRACTION
- GREEN
- GUATEMALA
- HOUSE
- IRISH
- KENYA
- MOCHA
- ORGANIC
- SMOOTH
- TASTE
- VIETNAM
- WHITE

127 Gardening

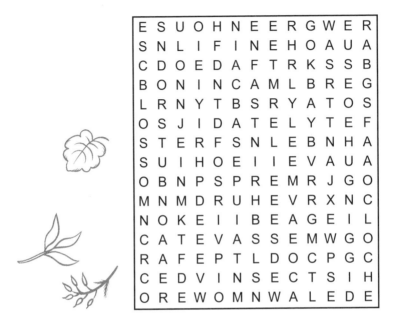

```
E S U O H N E E R G W E R
S N L I F I N E H O A U A
C D O E D A F T R K S S B
B O N I N C A M L B R E G
L R N Y T B S R Y A T O S
O S J I D A T E L Y T E F
S T E R F S N L E B N H A
S U I H O E I I E V A U A
O B N P S P R E M R J G O
M N M D R U H E V R X N C
N O K E I I B E A G E I L
C A T E V A S S E M W G O
R A F E P T L D O C P G C
C E D V I N S E C T S I H
O R E W O M N W A L E D E
```

- BEEHIVE
- BIRDBATH
- BLOSSOM
- BUSHES
- CATERPILLARS
- CLOCHE
- COMPOST
- CONIFER
- DIGGING
- FORK
- GERMINATION
- GREENHOUSE
- HARVEST
- INSECTS
- LAWNMOWER
- ROSES
- SUNDIAL
- WORMS

128 Happy

```
P L E Y E D E L L I R H T
B J A W K C I K O N E M D
Y L L O J C S H M A B A N
M P H U G A U T M T O J O
A M T N F R E L A N F U O
N E E R F E R A C T P S M
G R E A L S E L T U I T E
A Y D A K D O L P E G C H
N E T F N U Y B G D A N T
P E A U D K E S G E Z G R
D E C N R A U F D S E R E
T O I E T N A I D A R V V
J N P G N M L I V E L Y O
E R F Y T P U I U L T G E
L A I V O J J E L P Y I K
```

- CAREFREE
- ECSTATIC
- ELATED
- GLAD
- GLEEFUL
- JOCUND
- JOLLY
- JOVIAL
- LIVELY
- LUCKY
- ON CLOUD NINE
- OVER THE MOON
- PERKY
- PLEASED
- RADIANT
- SUNNY
- THRILLED
- UPBEAT

129 Ballets

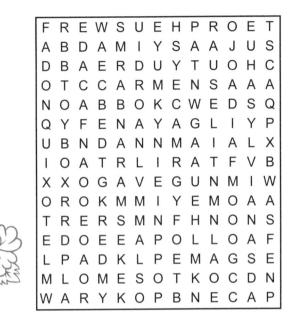

```
F R E W S U E H P R O E T
A B D A M I Y S A A J U S
D B A E R D U Y T U O H C
O T C C A R M E N S A A A
N O A B B O K C W E D S Q
Q Y F E N A Y A G L I Y P
U B N D A N N M A I A L X
I O A T R L I R A T F V B
X X O G A V E G U N M I W
O R O K M M I Y E M O A A
T R E R S M N F H N O N S
E D O E E A P O L L O A F
L P A D K L P E M A G S E
M L O M E S O T K O C D N
W A R Y K O P B N E C A P
```

- *AGON*
- *ANYUTA*
- *APOLLO*
- *BOLERO*
- *CARMEN*
- *CHOUT*

- *DON QUIXOTE*
- *FACADE*
- *GAYANE*
- *LA ESMERALDA*
- *MANON*
- *ONEGIN*

- *ORPHEUS*
- *RAYMONDA*
- *RODEO*
- *SWAN LAKE*
- *SYLVIA*
- *TOY BOX*

Solutions

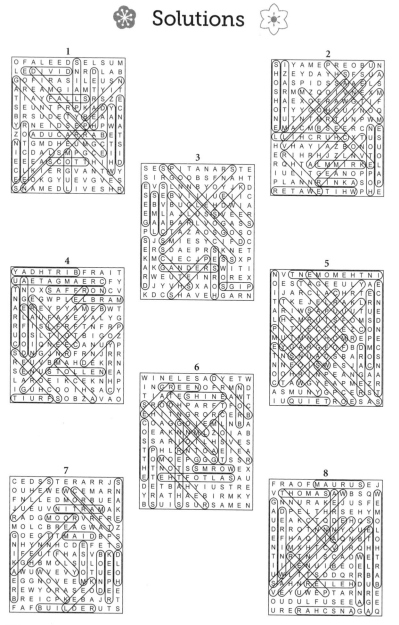

Solutions

9

10

11

12

13

14

15

16

Solutions

17

18

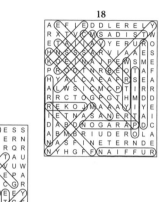

19

20

21

22

23

24

146

Solutions

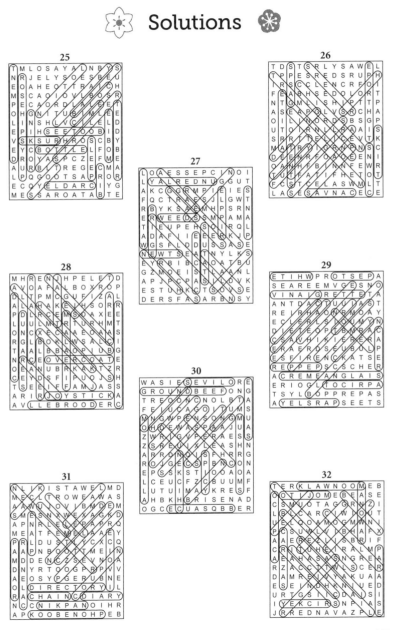

Solutions

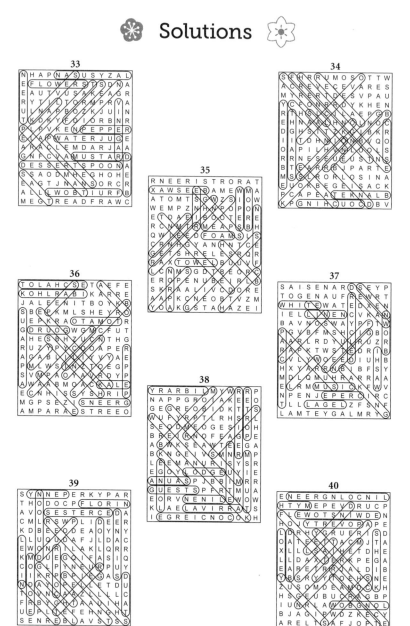

Solutions

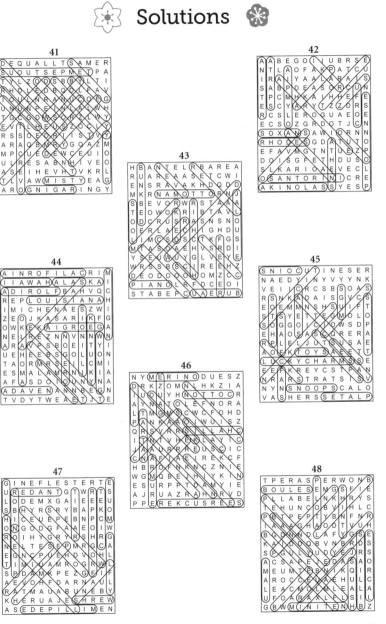

Solutions

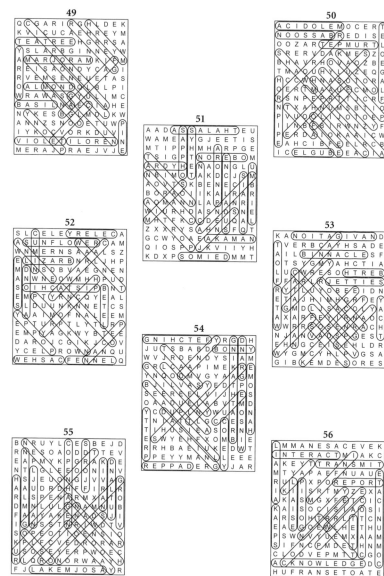

Solutions

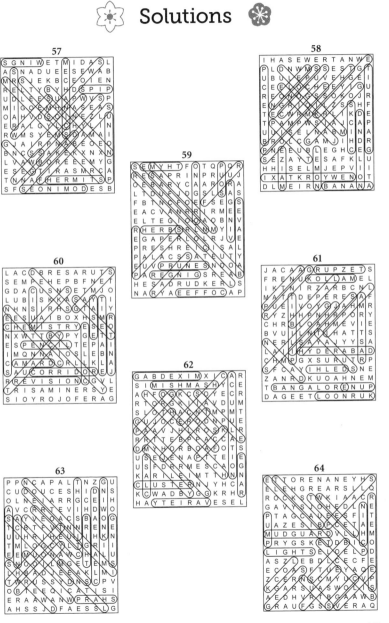

57

58

59

60

61

62

63

64

Solutions

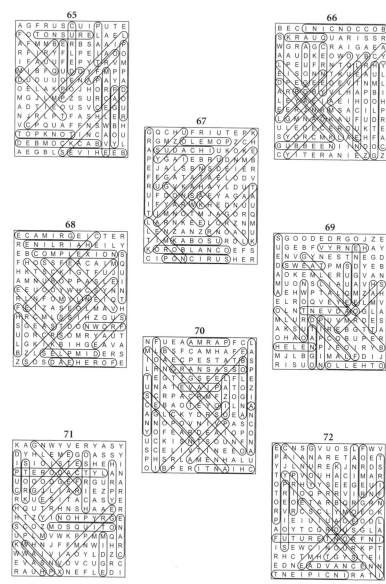

Solutions

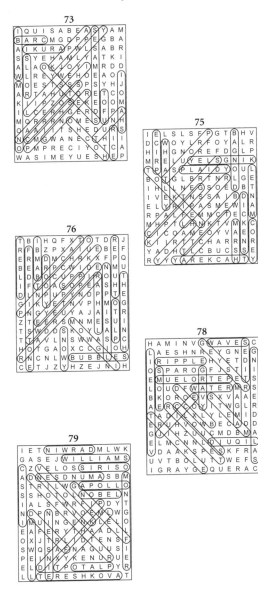

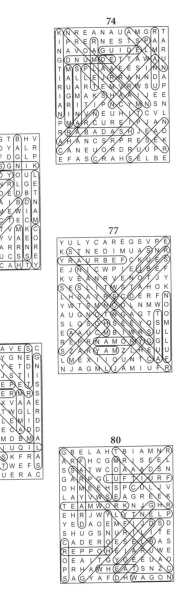

 **Solutions**

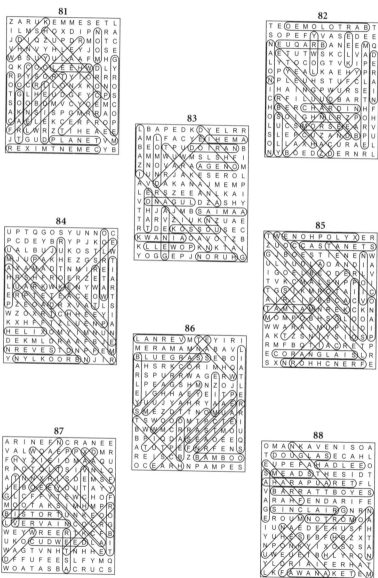

Solutions

89

90

91

92

93

94

95

96

Solutions

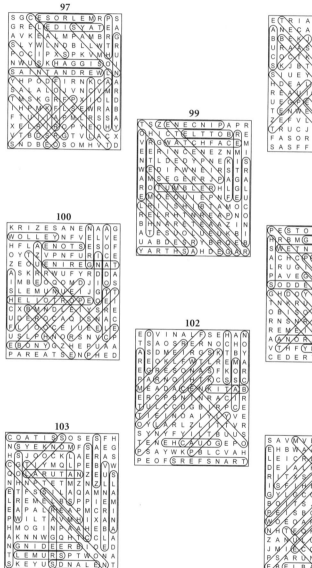

Solutions

105

106

107

108

109

110

111

112

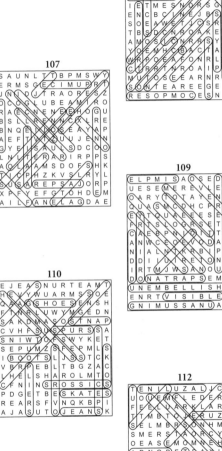

Solutions

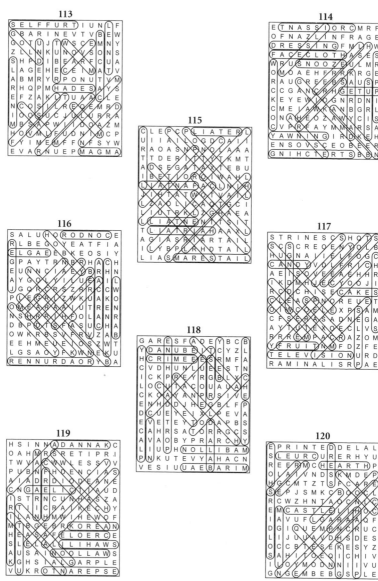

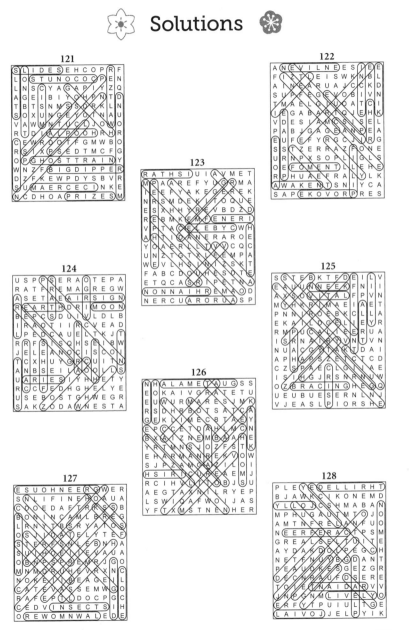

Solutions

129